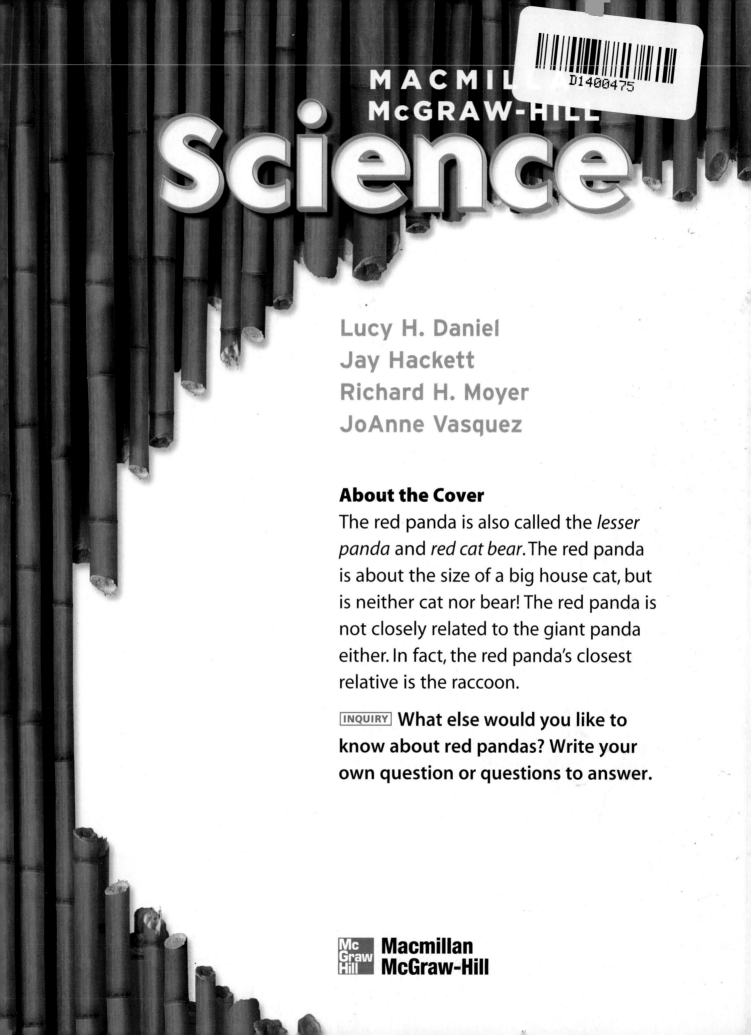

MACMILLAN McGRAW-HILL
Science

Lucy H. Daniel

Jay Hackett

Richard H. Moyer

JoAnne Vasquez

About the Cover

The red panda is also called the *lesser panda* and *red cat bear*. The red panda is about the size of a big house cat, but is neither cat nor bear! The red panda is not closely related to the giant panda either. In fact, the red panda's closest relative is the raccoon.

INQUIRY What else would you like to know about red pandas? Write your own question or questions to answer.

Macmillan
McGraw-Hill

Program Authors

Dr. Lucy H. Daniel
Teacher, Consultant
Rutherford County Schools, North Carolina

Dr. Jay Hackett
Professor Emeritus of Earth Sciences
University of Northern Colorado

Dr. Richard H. Moyer
Professor of Science Education
University of Michigan-Dearborn

Dr. JoAnne Vasquez
Elementary Science Education Consultant
Mesa Public Schools, Arizona
NSTA Past President

Contributing Authors

Lucille Villegas Barrera, M.Ed.
Elementary Science Supervisor
Houston Independent School District
Houston, Texas

Mulugheta Teferi, M.A.
St. Louis Public Schools
St. Louis, Missouri

Dinah Zike, M.Ed.
Dinah Might Adventures LP
San Antonio, Texas

The features in this textbook entitled "Amazing Stories," as well as the unit openers, were developed in collaboration with the National Geographic Society's School Publishing Division.

Copyright © 2002 National Geographic Society. All rights reserved.

RFB&D ⓥ
learning through listening

Students with print disabilities may be eligible to obtain an accessible, audio version of the pupil edition of this textbook. Please call Recording for the Blind & Dyslexic at 1-800-221-4792 for complete information.

The McGraw·Hill Companies

Macmillan McGraw-Hill

Published by Macmillan/McGraw-Hill, of McGraw-Hill Education, a division of The McGraw-Hill Companies, Inc., Two Penn Plaza, New York, New York 10121.

FOLDABLES is a trademark of The McGraw-Hill Companies, Inc.

Printed in the United States of America

ISBN 0-02-282595-9

5 6 7 8 9 110/043 09 08 07 06

Consultants

Dr. Carol Baskin
University of Kentucky
Lexington, KY

Dr. Joe W. Crim
University of Georgia
Athens, GA

Dr. Marie DiBerardino
Allegheny University of
Health Sciences
Philadelphia, PA

Dr. R. E. Duhrkopf
Baylor University
Waco, TX

Dr. Dennis L. Nelson
Montana State University
Bozeman, MT

Dr. Fred Sack
Ohio State University
Columbus, OH

Dr. Martin VanDyke
Denver, CO

Dr. E. Peter Volpe
Mercer University
Macon, GA

Consultants

Dr. Clarke Alexander
Skidaway Institute of
Oceanography
Savannah, GA

Dr. Suellen Cabe
Pembroke State University
Pembroke, NC

Dr. Thomas A. Davies
Texas A & M University
College Station, TX

Dr. Ed Geary
Geological Society of America
Boulder, CO

Dr. David C. Kopaska-Merkel
Geological Survey of Alabama
Tuscaloosa, AL

Consultants

Dr. Bonnie Buratti
Jet Propulsion Lab
Pasadena, CA

Dr. Shawn Carlson
Society of Amateur Scientists
San Diego, CA

Dr. Karen Kwitter
Williams College
Williamstown, MA

Dr. Steven Souza
Williamstown, MA

Dr. Joseph P. Straley
University of Kentucky
Lexington, KY

Dr. Thomas Troland
University of Kentucky
Lexington, KY

Dr. Josephine Davis Wallace
University of North Carolina
Charlotte, NC

Consultant for Primary Grades

Donna Harrell Lubcker
East Texas Baptist University
Marshall, TX

Teacher Reviewers (continued)

Beth Lewis
Wilmington, North Carolina

Cindy Hatchell
Wilmington, North Carolina

Cindy Kahler
Carrboro, North Carolina

Diane Leusky
Chapel Hill, North Carolina

Heather Sutton
Wilmington, North Carolina

Crystal Stephens
Valdese, North Carolina

Meg Millard
Chapel Hill, North Carolina

Patricia Underwood
Randleman, North Carolina

E. Joy Mermin
Chapel Hill, North Carolina

Yolanda Evans
Wilmington, North Carolina

Tim Gilbride
Pennsauken, New Jersey

Helene Reifowitz
Nesconsit, New York

Tina Craig
Tulsa, Oklahoma

Deborah Harwell
Lawton, Oklahoma

Kathleen Conn
West Chester, Pennsylvania

Heath Renninger Zerbe
Tremont, Pennsylvania

Patricia Armillei
Holland, Pennsylvania

Sue Workman
Cedar City, Utah

Peg Jensen
Hartford, Wisconsin

Cycles on Earth and in Space PAGE D1

Science Handbook

Health Handbook

Activities

Unit D

Explore Activities

Quick Labs with FOLDABLES™

Inquiry Skill Builders

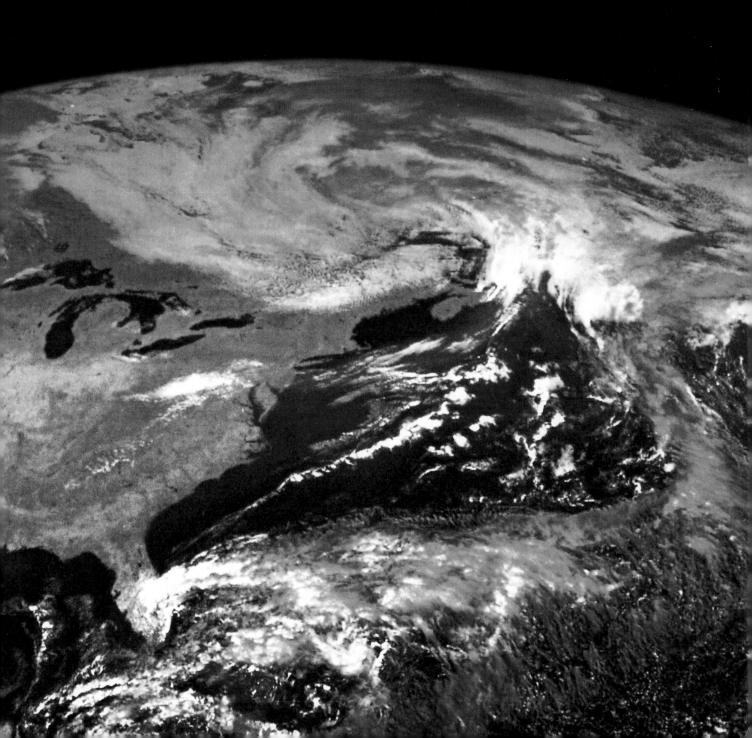

UNIT D

Cycles on Earth and in Space

Cycles on Earth and in Space

LOOK!

The Moon moves around Earth. How do you think Earth moves through space

Earth's Weather

Did You Ever Wonder?

How does snow form? Snow is not frozen rain. Snow forms when water in the gas state, called water vapor, changes directly into ice crystals. As the crystals fall to Earth, they combine to form snowflakes. No two snowflakes are alike.

INQUIRY SKILL Form a Hypothesis How does water get into the air?

Vocabulary

atmosphere, D6
weather, D6
temperature, D8
air pressure, D9

Get Ready

Here's a puzzle to solve. The picture may help you. Name something that is real but that you cannot see. Here's a hint. It's helping these kites fly. If you answered "Air," you are right.

How do you know air is real?

Inquiry Skill
You **communicate** when you share information.

Explore Activity

How Can You Show That Air Is Real?

Materials

plastic container

plastic cup

water

paper towels

Procedure

1. Fill the container about half full with water. Put a dry paper towel completely inside the cup.

2. Hold the cup upside down. Push the cup to the bottom of the container. Be careful not to tilt the cup.

3. **Observe** Remove the cup from the water. Remember to be careful not to tilt the cup. Look at the towel. Record your findings.

4. **Observe** Again, hold the cup upside down, and push it to the bottom of the container. This time slowly tilt the cup. Record your findings.

Drawing Conclusions

1. What happened to the towel in step 3? In step 4?

2. What keeps water from filling the cup?

3. Is air real? How can you tell?

4. FURTHER INQUIRY
   Communicate How would this activity work on the Moon? Explain.

Main Idea Three characteristics of the weather are air temperature, air pressure, and wind.

Where Is Air?

You cannot taste, smell, or see air. So, how can you tell if air is real? Wave a plastic sandwich bag around, and close it. There is something in the bag. That something is air.

Air is all around you. Air surrounds the entire Earth. The air that surrounds Earth is called the **atmosphere** (AT·muhs·feer). The atmosphere is made up of different gases and dust. Some of the dust comes from fires and volcanoes on Earth.

What do we know about Earth's atmosphere? It is made up of layers. Each layer has its own characteristics. The layer closest to the surface of Earth is called the *troposphere* (TRAHP·uh·sfeer). All life on Earth exists here. This is where **weather** (WETH·uhr) takes place. Weather is what the air is like at a given time and place.

▷ **What makes up the atmosphere?**

Layers of the Atmosphere

Thermosphere
The thermosphere is the top layer of the atmosphere. Light displays called the *northern lights* happen here.

Mesosphere
The mesosphere is between the stratosphere and the thermosphere.

Stratosphere
In the stratosphere the air is not still. Very strong winds called the *jet stream* are located here.

Troposphere
The troposphere is the layer of the atmosphere closest to Earth. In this layer clouds, rain, snow, and thunderstorms occur.

READING
Diagrams

1. Which layer is the airplane in?

2. Where does weather take place?

What Is Air Temperature?

What do you say when you go outside on a hot summer day? You say, "It is hot." The *it* is the air.

The Sun heats the air, so it feels hot. It has a high **temperature** (TEM·puhr·uh·chuhr). Temperature is a measure of how hot or cold something is. The Sun also heats Earth's surface—both the land and the water.

Air temperature is always changing. You know that it is usually warmer during the day than at night. The Sun heats Earth and the air.

How can you measure temperature? You need to use a *thermometer*. The diagram at the right shows you how to read a thermometer.

Does all the air around Earth get the same amount of heat from the Sun? Not really. Places near Earth's North and South Poles do not get as much sunlight as places near the equator. The Sun stays low in the sky near the poles. This is one reason why it is warmer near the equator than near the poles.

▷ **What heats the air?**

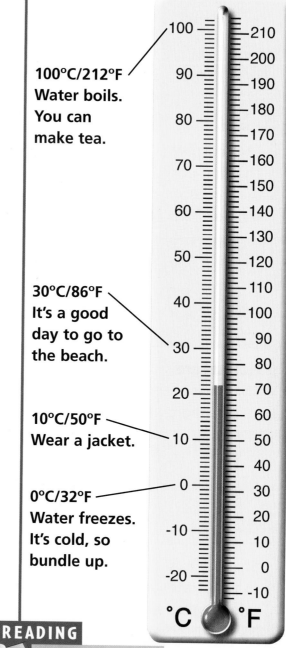

Measuring Air Temperature

100°C/212°F Water boils. You can make tea.

30°C/86°F It's a good day to go to the beach.

10°C/50°F Wear a jacket.

0°C/32°F Water freezes. It's cold, so bundle up.

°C °F

READING Diagrams

1. When would you wear a jacket?

2. At what temperature does water freeze?

What Is Air Pressure?

The weight of the atmosphere presses on you all the time. It presses on everything on Earth. The pressing down force of the air on Earth is called **air pressure**.

Do you feel air pressure? Not usually. Your body is used to air pressure. You don't even notice it most of the time. However, you can notice when air pressure changes. What happens when you drive up mountain roads? Your ears "pop." This pop is caused by a change in air pressure pushing on your eardrum. You may also feel your ears pop if you ride in an elevator or fly in an airplane.

▷ **What is air pressure?**

As climbers scale a mountain, the air pressure changes.

QUICK LAB

Mighty Air

FOLDABLES™ Make a Two-Tab Book. (See p. R41.) Mark the book as shown.

1. Place a ruler on a desk. Half of the ruler should be hanging off the edge of the desk. Draw the set-up on the left tab.

2. **Observe** Carefully hit the edge of the ruler that is hanging off the desk with your hand. What happens? Record your answer under the left tab.

3. Cover the ruler with a page of newspaper. Draw the set-up on the right tab.

4. **Predict** What do you think will happen when the ruler is hit? Record your predictions on the right tab.

5. **Observe** Hit the ruler again. What happens? Write down your findings under the right tab.

What Happens When Air Moves?

Air moves from an area of high pressure to an area of lower pressure. This moving air is called *wind.*

What if you pour two cups of water toward each other in a sink? What happens when they meet? The water mixes and may even churn and bubble. When two different bodies of air meet, they also mix. Large bodies of air are called air masses. The place where different masses of air meet is where most weather changes happen. Here it may be cloudy or rainy or stormy.

A windsock is a common sight at an airport. It measures the direction of the wind.

READING Summarize
What happens when two different air masses meet?

The Movement of Air

A sea breeze blows from the water onto the shore. It occurs during the day when the air over the water is cooler than the air over the land. Cooler air has higher pressure. Air moves from an area of high pressure to an area of lower pressure.

A land breeze blows from the land onto the water. It occurs during the night when the air over the land is cooler than the air over the water. Cooler air has higher pressure. Air moves from an area of high pressure to an area of lower pressure.

Why It Matters

Weather changes from day to day. Weather also changes over the course of the seasons. Weather can be observed by measuring temperature. Weather can also be observed by describing cloud formations.

e-Journal Visit our Web site www.science.mmhschool.com to do a research project on weather.

Think and Write

1. Name two properties of air.

2. What do you use to measure temperature?

3. What is air pressure?

4. What is wind?

5. **Critical Thinking** How can changes in the weather affect your day?

L·I·N·K·S

WRITING LINK

Expository Writing Observe the weather in your area for a week. Measure the air temperature with a thermometer. Also, describe the cloud formations. Write down your notes in your journal. Use your findings to write a report.

MATH LINK

Make a data chart. Use research materials or the Internet to find the average monthly temperature where you live. Record the information for each month of the year on a chart. What do you notice about the temperature patterns throughout the year?

ART LINK

Create a weather picture. People often say it is raining "cats and dogs" when it is raining very hard. Draw a picture of some strange weather. Write a few sentences to describe your picture.

TECHNOLOGY LINK

LOG ON Visit www.science.mmhschool.com for more links.

Extreme Weather

Have you been through a hurricane? a flood? a tornado? If you have, you'll never forget it.

Tornadoes, hurricanes, and floods are natural disasters. They can destroy roads, bridges, homes, and schools. It is important to know when events like these are coming. They can be dangerous!

Tornadoes form on hot summer days. Thunderstorms whip air high up into the clouds. The rushing air spins rapidly as it rises. The spinning winds can reach 300 miles per hour! A tornado this strong will destroy anything in its path. It can pick up a car and throw it blocks away! The best way to protect yourself is to go below ground.

Hurricanes are the largest storms on Earth. Circular winds form over the ocean. As they move over warm water, they get stronger. Scientists can track a hurricane for weeks. That gives people several days to prepare.

Powerful winds can destroy everything in their path.

Weather satellite photos like this one can track hurricanes and give people time to get out of the way.

A hurricane's fierce winds can knock out electricity. Its heavy rains can turn roads into rivers. People should leave low lying areas. They should store bottled water, canned food, and fresh batteries for flashlights and radios.

Floods are the most common of all natural disasters. They can be caused by heavy rains or melting snow. Rivers and streams overflow their banks. Water rushes through low-lying areas. Sometimes floods can help by bringing rich soil to farmlands. But nobody wants to see homes washed away or buried under mud!

Write About It

1. How should you prepare for a hurricane?

2. Where is the safest place to go if a tornado is near?

LOG ON Visit **www.science.mmschool.com** to learn more about extreme weather.

The Water Cycle

Get Ready

Can you see all of the Golden Gate Bridge? Where do you think the fog that hides it came from? Fog is a cloud that forms near the ground. What are clouds made of?

Inquiry Skill

You make a model when you make something to represent an object or event.

Explore Activity

How Do Raindrops Form?

Materials

clear-plastic jar

plastic wrap

rubber band

marble

ice cubes

warm water

Procedure

1. Fill the jar one-fourth full of warm water.

2. Place plastic wrap over the top of the jar. Use a rubber band to seal the wrap to the jar.

3. Set a marble in the center of the plastic wrap.

4. **Make a Model** Place several small pieces of ice on top of the plastic wrap. You have made a model of Earth. The warm water represents a lake, and the air above it represents the air around Earth.

5. **Observe** Carefully watch the bottom of the plastic wrap. Record your observations.

Drawing Conclusions

1. What did you see inside the jar?

2. Where did the water come from to make the raindrops?

3. **Infer** Do you think water might go into the air faster during the day or the night? Why?

4. FURTHER INQUIRY **Infer** What do you think would have happened if you had poured cold water into the jar instead of warm water? Try it.

Main Idea The water cycle is the path water follows on Earth.

Where Does Water Go?

Have you ever seen tiny droplets of water on a bathroom mirror? Where did the droplets come from? Are you surprised to learn that they came from the air?

Everything around you is made up of something called *matter*. Air, water, and this book are all made of matter. Matter can be found in three different forms—solid, liquid, and gas.

A solid is a form of matter that has a definite shape and takes up a definite amount of space. A book is an example of a solid.

A liquid takes up a definite amount of space but does not have a definite shape. A liquid takes the shape of its container. This pitcher of juice is a liquid.

A gas has no definite size or shape. It spreads out to fill the container that holds it. Think of a balloon. The air inside the balloon spreads out to fill the entire balloon.

This journal is a solid.

The juice in this pitcher is a liquid.

Inside this balloon is helium. Helium is a gas.

Water is matter that can be a solid, a liquid, or a gas. How can you change the form of matter?

After it rains, there are puddles in the street. The next day they are gone. Where did the water go? The water went into the air above. When this happens, the water changes. It changes from a liquid into a gas. This gas is **water vapor**. The changing of a liquid into a gas is called **evaporation** (i·vap·uh·RAY·shuhn).

Have you ever seen water droplets on the inside of a window? These water droplets did not come from rain. They came from the air itself! When water vapor in the air cools, it changes back into liquid water. The change of a gas into a liquid is called **condensation** (kahn·den·SAY·shuhn).

Where did the water droplets on this web come from?

READING **Summarize**
What happens during the process of evaporation?

Where might the water in this lake go?

What Is the Water Cycle?

Animals and plants use water every day to survive. Where do they get the water they need? They get the water from one or more parts of the **water cycle**. The water cycle is the never-ending path water takes between Earth and the atmosphere.

The Water Cycle

Water condenses
As water vapor rises into the air, it cools. The cooled water vapor changes back into liquid water drops. The liquid water drops form clouds.

Water evaporates
The Sun heats the water in the oceans and on land. The water changes from a liquid into water vapor.

Water evaporates into the air, condenses into clouds, and returns to Earth as **precipitation** (pri·sip·i·TAY·shuhn). Precipitation is water that returns to Earth from the atmosphere. It can be in the form of rain, snow, sleet, or hail.

▶ **What is the water cycle?**

Precipitation
When enough water has condensed in clouds, the water falls to Earth as precipitation. Precipitation can be in the form of rain, snow, sleet, or hail. The form of precipitation depends mainly on the temperature.

Water on the ground
Some precipitation flows downhill into lakes, rivers, and oceans. Some falls directly into these bodies of water. Some precipitation soaks into the ground. This water is called *groundwater*.

READING Diagrams

1. What part of the water cycle is easy to see?

2. Why is this path of water called a cycle?

Inquiry Skill
BUILDER

 **SKILL** Make a Model and Infer

How Does Temperature Affect Evaporation?

Does the temperature of the air affect evaporation? How could you find out? In this activity you will make a model and then infer to investigate this question.

Materials

water

2 plastic cups

marker

Procedure

1 **Make a Model** Fill each cup half full with water. Use the marker to show where the water level is.

2 Place one cup in a warm place. Place the other cup in a cool place.

3 **Predict** In which cup will the water level change the most? Record your prediction.

4 **Observe** Look at the cups every day for one week. Measure the water depth in the cups. Record your measurements. How did the amount of water change?

Drawing Conclusions

1 **Infer** Where did the water go?

2 How did the amount of water differ after two days?

3 How does this compare with your prediction?

4 **Infer** How could you use this model to make seawater drinkable?

L·I·N·K·S

Why It Matters

Water is one of our most important resources. You need to drink fresh water every day. Plants and animals need water, too. The water cycle is nature's way of recycling. The continuous movement of water through the water cycle provides us with fresh, clean water.

e-Journal Visit our Web site www.science.mmhschool.com to do a research project on the water cycle.

Think and Write

1. What is water vapor?

2. Why does a puddle seem to disappear?

3. What determines whether precipitation is rain or snow?

4. **INQUIRY SKILL** **Make a Model** Draw a picture to show evaporation and condensation.

5. **Critical Thinking** What do you think might happen if there were no water cycle?

MATH LINK

Solve a problem. Ten inches of snow is approximately equal to one inch of rain. If it snowed five inches, how much rain would that be?

ART LINK

Create a poster. Make a list of the different ways you can use water. Then find or draw pictures of these ways. Use them to make a poster.

WRITING LINK

Writing a Poem Write the words *water cycle* in a word ladder down the side of a sheet of paper. Think of words that describe the water cycle and that begin with each letter in the two words. Arrange these words into a poem.

TECHNOLOGY LINK

LOG ON Visit www.science.mmhschool.com for more links.

Describing Weather

Get Ready

Look outside. Is it sunny? Is it raining? When you were outside, how did it feel? What is the weather like where you live? How do you measure the conditions of the air? For example, how can you measure air temperature?

Inquiry Skill

You measure when you find the temperature and air pressure.

Explore Activity

Materials

thermometer

How Do You Measure Temperature?

Procedure

1 **Predict** Where do you think the air temperature in your classroom is the highest and the lowest? Record your predictions.

2 **Measure** Use a thermometer to find the air temperature at several places in the classroom. Then read and record the temperature. Remember to include the places in your predictions.

3 How did your measurements compare with your predictions?

Drawing Conclusions

1 What was the warmest spot in your classroom? What was the coolest spot in your classroom?

2 **Communicate** Use the measurements to make a bar graph.

3 FURTHER INQUIRY **Predict** What if you were doing this activity outside? Predict where you think the air temperature would be the highest and the lowest. Test your predictions.

Main Idea Temperature, air pressure, and wind speed can be measured.

How Do You Describe Weather?

When scientists describe weather, they measure temperature, air pressure, and amount of precipitation. They also measure the speed and direction of the wind.

You measure the temperature of the air with a thermometer. These pictures show the main weather instruments and what they measure.

A **thermometer** (thuhr·MAHM·i·tuhr) measures the temperature of the air. Indoor-outdoor thermometers give the air temperature both inside the house and outside at the same time.

A *rain gauge* measures how much precipitation has fallen.

A **barometer** (buh·RAHM·i·tuhr) measures air pressure. If the reading on the barometer is rising, it usually means fair weather is coming. A falling barometer reading usually means precipitation is on its way.

READING Summarize
What instruments do you use to describe weather?

A *weather vane* indicates the direction of the wind. The arrowhead tells you where the wind is coming from.

An *anemometer* (an·uh·MAHM·i·tuhr) measures how fast the air is moving. It gives you the wind's speed.

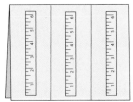
Make a Rain Gauge

FOLDABLES™ Make a Three-Tab Book. (See p. R43.) Mark the book as shown.

1. Use a plastic jar as a rain gauge. Tape a six-inch paper ruler to the jar. Make sure the ruler is straight up and down. Zero should be at the bottom of the jar.

2. When it is going to rain, place your jar in an open area where it can collect rain. Don't put the jar near or under trees or near buildings.

3. **Observe** After it rains, see how much rain fell. Try to measure to the nearest eighth of an inch.

4. **Measure** Record the amount of rainfall on your Foldables book. Do this for several rains.

How Do You Read a Weather Map?

What do you do when you make observations? You write them down. You might also share your data with other people.

Scientists gather data about the weather. They use symbols to show the data on a large weather map. The map shows weather conditions over a large area. Scientists then share this information with others and make weather forecasts.

Look at the weather map of the United States below. This weather map shows you cloud cover, temperature, and other current weather conditions. Some places, such as Phoenix, are having hot, sunny weather. Other places, such as New York City, are cooler and rainy. Each color band represents an area where the temperature falls in the same range.

▷ **What does a weather map show?**

READING
Maps

1. What is the current temperature for Phoenix, Arizona?

2. What is the current cloud cover for Atlanta, Georgia?

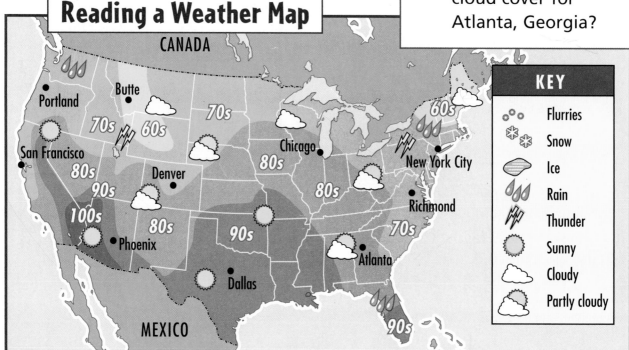

Reading a Weather Map

CANADA

Portland · Butte · 70s 60s

70s

San Francisco · 80s Denver · Chicago · 80s New York City 60s

90s 80s Richmond

100s 80s 90s 80s 70s

· Phoenix

Dallas · 90s Atlanta 70s

MEXICO 90s

KEY

Flurries
Snow
Ice
Rain
Thunder
Sunny
Cloudy
Partly cloudy

Lesson Review

Why It Matters

Weather patterns are constantly changing. That is why being able to read a weather map is important. For example, if you see that cities west of you are having rain, you'll probably have rain the next day. This can help you decide what to wear and what to do.

e-Journal Visit our Web site www.science.mmhschool.com to do a research project on weather pattern and changes.

Think and Write

1. How do you measure temperature?

2. What does a barometer measure?

3. Name two other weather instruments. What do they measure?

4. What information does a weather map provide?

5. **Critical Thinking** How might you use the information from a weather report?

L·I·N·K·S

LITERATURE LINK

Read *Stormy Weather* to learn about the weather. When you finish reading, list some of the kinds of weather in the story. Try the activities at the end of the book.

WRITING LINK

Expository Writing This weather-satellite photo shows a hurricane. Some areas of the United States have more hurricanes than others. Do research to find out which U.S. regions have the most hurricanes. Explain why in an essay.

MATH LINK

Make a bar graph. Use the Internet to gather data on the average annual rainfall for five different cities. Record the average annual rainfall for each city in a table. Use the table to make a bar graph.

TECHNOLOGY LINK

 LOG ON Visit www.science.mmhschool.com for more links.

The Ups and Downs of Tides

If you live near the ocean, you probably know about tides. Tides are the rise and fall of the ocean's water level. Places along the ocean's shore usually have two high tides each day. The water level is high, and the edge of the ocean moves inland. In between high tides are low tides. The water level is low, and the edge of the ocean moves back out.

What causes tides? The answer comes from outer space! The Moon's gravity causes the oceans to bulge in some places and shrink in others. Because the Moon and Earth are always moving, tides rise and fall every day. Gravity from the Sun also affects tides.

At some places along the shore, you can find tide pools. Tide pools are puddles of water that a high tide leaves behind. It's fun to explore tide pools. You might find sea stars, crabs, or other sea creatures.

It is high tide. The water level is high.

It is low tide. Look at what happened to the water level.

People can find shells and interesting sea creatures in tide pools.

Write ABOUT IT

1. What causes tides to rise and fall?
2. How might tides affect the lives of people who live by the ocean?

LOG ON Visit www.science.mmhschool.com to learn more about tides.

Chapter 7 Review

Vocabulary

Fill each blank with the best word or words from the list.

air pressure, D9   **precipitation,** D19

atmosphere, D6   **temperature,** D8

barometer, D24   **thermometer,** D24

condensation,   **water vapor,** D17
D17
            weather, D6

evaporation, D17

1. The air around Earth is a mixture of gases and dust called the _____.

2. The _____ of something measures how hot or cold it is.

3. The force of air pushing down on Earth is called _____.

4. Water in a gas form is called _____.

5. Rain, snow, hail, and sleet fall to Earth and are called _____.

6. A tool used to measure air pressure is a(n) _____.

7. The condition of the atmosphere at a given time and place is the _____.

8. To measure air temperature, you would use a(n) _____.

The water cycle is a never-ending process of precipitation,

9. _____

10. _____.

Test Prep

11. In which layer of the atmosphere does all weather take place?

    A troposphere

    B stratosphere

    C ozone

    D outer space

12. The change from a gas into a liquid is _____.

    F evaporation

    G condensation

    H precipitation

    J runoff

13. A weather map shows _____.

    A temperature ranges

    B cloud cover

    C precipitation

    D all of the above

14. A weather vane is used to measure _____.

   F wind

   G rainfall

   H temperature

   J air pressure

15. After it rains, some water soaks into the ground to become _____.

   A water vapor

   B groundwater

   C runoff

   D precipitation

Concepts and Skills

16. **Reading in Science** Study the drawing. Describe how water moves through the water cycle. Use the words *evaporation*, *condensation*, and *precipitation* in your answer.

17. **Critical Thinking** Air pressure is lower on mountains than in valleys. Why do you think this is so?

18. **INQUIRY SKILL** **Infer** If you pour lemonade into a cold glass, drops of water form outside the glass. What causes the drops to form?

19. **Scientific Methods** For the past two weeks, what was the average temperature in your town? Use the Internet to answer this question.

20. **Decision Making** Pretend you're a farmer. Fall has arrived and you need to harvest your crops. How does the weather affect you? What decisions might you make based on the weather?

Did You Ever Wonder?

INQUIRY SKILL **Predict** You have seen what causes weather to change. Gather information and predict your local weather for a week. Test your predictions.

LOG ON Visit **www.science.mmhschool.com** to boost your test scores.

Earth in Space

Did You Ever Wonder?

How do scientists learn about space? One way is to
look at the night sky through a telescope. Powerful
telescopes are put in buildings called observatories.
Observatories are often built on mountains or
hilltops, away from the lights of cities.

INQUIRY SKILL **Communicate** What do we know
about the objects in space?

D 32

How Earth Moves

Vocabulary

sphere, D36
rotate, D36
axis, D37
revolve, D38
orbit, D38

Get Ready

Have you ever watched the Sun set and turn day into night? Have you watched the Sun rise? A dark sky brightens with just a peek of the Sun. What do you think causes night and day?

Inquiry Skill

You **make a model** when you make something to represent an object or event.

D 34

Explore Activity

What Causes Day and Night?

Materials

globe

medium self-stick notes

flashlight

Procedure

1 Write *I live here* on a self-stick note. Place the note over the United States on the globe. While one person holds the globe, shine the flashlight on the self-stick note.

2 **Observe** If the flashlight is the Sun, would it be day or night on the self-stick note? Is it day or night on the other side of the globe?

3 Think of two different ways to make it night at the place near the self-stick note.

4 **Make a Model** Use the globe and the flashlight to test your ideas.

Drawing Conclusions

1 How did you create day and night in the first model and in the second model?

2 Which idea do you think better explains what you know about day and night? Why?

3 FURTHER INQUIRY **Infer** You put your wet sneakers in sunlight to dry. An hour later they are in shade. How do you know what happened? Use your model to explain.

Main Idea Earth's rotation causes day and night, and its revolution causes the seasons.

What Causes Day and Night?

A long time ago, people thought that Earth stood still while the Sun traveled around it each day. It's easy to see why people once thought the Sun moved. Every day we see the Sun seem to come up, move across the sky, and go down. Today we know that the Sun does not move around Earth.

Better instruments have helped us observe the movements of Earth. It is the movement of Earth that causes day and night. Earth is shaped like a ball. This shape is called a **sphere** (SFEER). Earth **rotates** (ROH·taytz). To rotate means to turn. As Earth rotates, there is daylight where Earth faces the Sun and darkness where Earth is turned away from the Sun.

The Rotating Earth

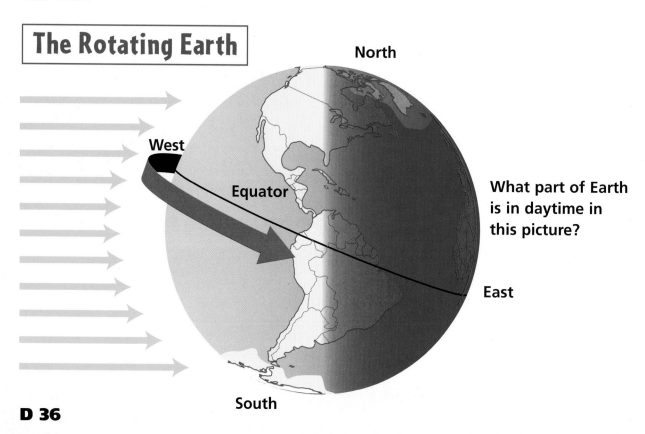

North

West

Equator

What part of Earth is in daytime in this picture?

East

South

It takes 24 hours for Earth to make one complete rotation. One complete rotation is one day. A day is made up of the hours of light and the hours of dark.

Look at the illustration below. Notice the line drawn through the center of Earth. This imaginary line is called an **axis** (AK·sis). Earth spins, or rotates, around its axis. As you can see, Earth's axis is not straight up and down. It is slightly tilted. At the north end of Earth's axis is the North Pole. At the south end is the South Pole.

The tilt of Earth changes how the Sun's rays strike the surface. At the poles the Sun stays low in the sky during the day. Here the Sun's rays are weak. This is why it is cold at the poles. At the equator the Sun rises high in the sky during the day. These rays are stronger. Here the air temperature is higher.

What is an axis?

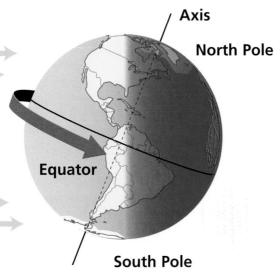

Axis

North Pole

Equator

South Pole

This tortoise lives near the equator. The temperature is warmer here.

These penguins live near the South Pole. The temperature is colder here.

What Causes the Seasons?

Rotation is only one way in which Earth moves. Earth also **revolves** (ri·VAHLVZ). An object that moves around another object revolves. Earth travels in a regular path around the Sun. It travels in an **orbit** (AWR·bit). An orbit is the path that an object follows as it revolves around another object. It takes one year, or $365\frac{1}{4}$ days, for Earth to make one complete revolution around the Sun.

In many parts of the world, the year is made up of four seasons—winter, spring, summer, and fall. Why do we have seasons? The answer has to do with Earth's tilted axis. Having a tilted axis means that Earth slants a little as it revolves around the Sun.

Look at the diagram. Notice that Earth is always tilted in the same direction. As Earth travels around the Sun, the part of Earth tilted toward the Sun changes. For part of the year, the North Pole tilts toward the Sun. During another part of the year, the North Pole tilts away from the Sun.

Summer
(begins June 21–22)
North America is tilted toward the Sun. The Sun is higher overhead, days are longer, and the temperature is warmer.

READING

Diagrams

If it is summer in the northern half of Earth, what season is it in the southern half?

When the North Pole is tilted toward the Sun, the Sun travels higher overhead in the sky. The Sun's rays shine straighter down on that part of Earth. It is then summer in that part of Earth. When the North Pole is tilted away from the Sun, the Sun stays lower in the sky. It is then winter in that part of Earth.

Earth Revolves Around the Sun

? What is a year?

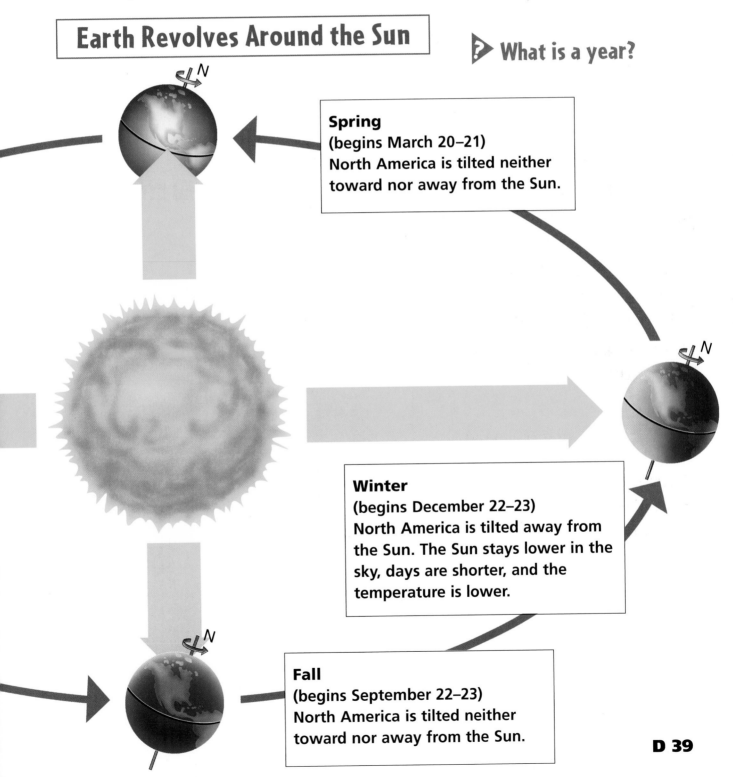

Spring
(begins March 20–21)
North America is tilted neither toward nor away from the Sun.

Winter
(begins December 22–23)
North America is tilted away from the Sun. The Sun stays lower in the sky, days are shorter, and the temperature is lower.

Fall
(begins September 22–23)
North America is tilted neither toward nor away from the Sun.

QUICK LAB

Sundial

FOLDABLES™ Make a Three-Tab Book. (See p. R43.) Mark the book as shown.

| 9:00 A.M. | 12:00 P.M. | 3:00 P.M. |

1. Tape a piece of paper to some cardboard. Use clay to anchor a pencil straight up at the center of the paper. Take your sundial outside at 9 A.M. on a sunny morning.

2. **Measure** Use a marker to draw a line through the middle of the pencil's shadow. Label the line with the time of day. Measure and mark the pencil's shadow again at 12 noon and 3 P.M.

3. On each tab of the Foldables book, draw the Sun's position.

4. How does the shadow's position change in one day? Is the Sun high or low in the sky when the shadows are the longest? Explain your answer on the back of your Foldables book.

How Does the Sun's Path in the Sky Change?

As the seasons change, so does the way the Sun appears to travel across the sky each day. In summer your part of Earth is tilted toward the Sun. The Sun's path appears higher in the sky. In winter your part of Earth is tilted away from the Sun. The Sun's path appears lower in the sky.

READING **Cause and Effect**
What causes the Sun to appear higher in the sky during the summer?

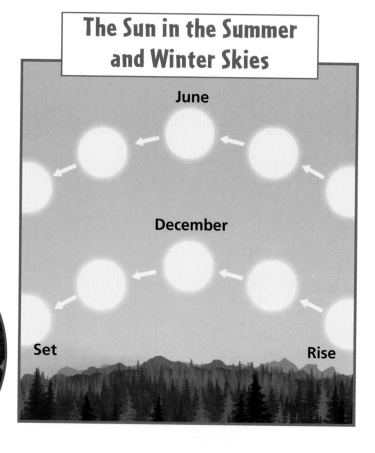

The Sun in the Summer and Winter Skies

June

December

Set   Rise

Why It Matters

The way Earth moves affects the way we lead our lives. Just think of all the things you do during the day and those you do at night. Also think about what you do throughout the year. Do you have a favorite season? Do you enjoy hot summer days, or do you like cooler ones?

 e-Journal Visit our Web site **www.science.mmhschool.com** to do a research project on the changing seasons.

Think and Write

1. If it is nighttime at a certain place on Earth, is that place facing toward or away from the Sun?

2. Describe the motion of Earth that makes up one day.

3. How are rotating and revolving different?

4. What would happen to the seasons if Earth's axis were not tilted?

5. **Critical Thinking** How would your life be different if you lived in the southern half of Earth?

L·I·N·K·S

MATH LINK

Solve a problem. You learned that the revolution of Earth around the Sun causes the four seasons. If each season is about the same number of months, about how many months long is each season? How can you tell?

HEALTH LINK

Conduct an interview. Ultraviolet (ul·truh·VIGH·uh·lit) light (UV) from the Sun causes a suntan or sunburn. Interview adult family members to find out how they protect their skin. Write down what they tell you.

WRITING LINK

Writing That Compares Describe how your life would change if Earth made one complete rotation every 12 hours. Compare and contrast this with 24 hours in your real life on Earth.

TECHNOLOGY LINK

 Science Newsroom CD-ROM Choose *Around the World* to learn how Earth's position affects the seasons.

LOG ON Visit **www.science.mmhschool.com** for more links.

Star Time

Can you tell time without a clock or a calendar? Yes, you can—by using the Sun and the stars!

Thousands of years ago, that's just what people did. Farmers used the position of the stars to tell the time of year.

Stargazers noticed that stars moved together across the sky. They also observed that stars were not evenly scattered. Some groups of brighter stars reminded people of familiar things – a lion, a hunter, a bull, a scorpion. We call these groups of stars constellations. As the seasons change, the constellations move across the sky.

Look at the sky at 8 p.m. one clear winter evening. Find the constellation Orion, the hunter. Check it again after one hour. Why is Orion moving? It's not! Earth is rotating, and you're on Earth. So you're the one who's moving!

The constellation Orion, the hunter.

Orion will be in a slightly different spot each night. This is because Earth is traveling around the Sun. As Earth moves, your view of the sky changes. In late spring, Orion disappears below the horizon. During the summer you'll see other constellations, such as Leo, the lion. But you won't see Orion again until late fall. In one year, Earth will circle the Sun once. Then Orion will be back in the same place in the sky.

Even today, our units of time are linked to the motions of our planet. The time it takes for Earth to rotate once is called one day. We break that day into parts—hours, minutes, and seconds. The time it takes Earth to revolve once around the Sun is called one year. The calendar is a daily reminder that we live on a planet!

Some stars are brighter than others.

What Did I Learn?

1. What did ancient people use to predict the seasons?

   A rocks
   B stars
   C animals
   D plants

2. Why do the stars appear to move across the sky at night?

   F Earth is rotating.
   G Orion, the hunter, is chasing them.
   H The stars don't appear to move.
   J The constellations are revolving around the Sun.

LOG ON Visit www.science.mmhschool.com to learn more about astronomy.

Phases of the Moon

Get Ready

Have you ever seen the Moon when it looked like this? Although the Moon is in the sky each day, it doesn't always look the same. Sometimes it is a full circle, and sometimes it is a thin slice. Why does the Moon seem to change shape?

Inquiry Skill

You **communicate** when you share information.

Explore Activity

Materials

lamp

volleyball

Why Does the Moon's Shape Change?

Procedure

1 **Observe** From your seat, look at the ball closely. Draw the ball.

2 **Make a Model** Turn off the classroom lights. Turn on the lamp, and shine it on one side of the ball. Draw the shape of the ball where the light hits it.

3 **Infer** Compare all the drawings. What do you think caused the different shapes?

Drawing Conclusions

1 How did the ball look when you first observed it? How did it look in the darkened room?

2 Why did your classmates see different lighted shapes?

3 **Infer** In this model the ball is the Moon and the lamp is the Sun. What are you?

4 **FURTHER INQUIRY**
Infer Why does the Moon appear to change its shape? How do you know?

How Does the Moon's Shape Change?

Each day the Moon seems to change shape. Sometimes you can see only a small part of the Moon. Other times it is a big, bright circle. Still other times you can't see it at all. The Moon is a **satellite** (SAT·uh·light) of Earth. A satellite is anything that orbits another, larger object in space. Half of the Moon always faces toward the Sun. The other half always faces away from the Sun.

The Moon, like a ball, is a sphere. The Moon does not change shape. It only appears to change shape because you see different amounts of its lighted part as it orbits Earth. The positions of the Sun and the Moon make it seem to change shape.

As the Moon orbits Earth, our view of it changes. The Moon appears to have different shapes. These changing shapes are called the Moon's **phases** (FAYZ·uhz). It takes about 29 days for the Moon to pass through all of its phases. Then the phases repeat. The four main phases of the Moon are new Moon, first quarter, full Moon, and last quarter.

The Moon rises and sets almost an hour later each day. Because of this we sometimes see the Moon in the daytime sky as well as at night.

▷ **Why does the Moon appear to change shape?**

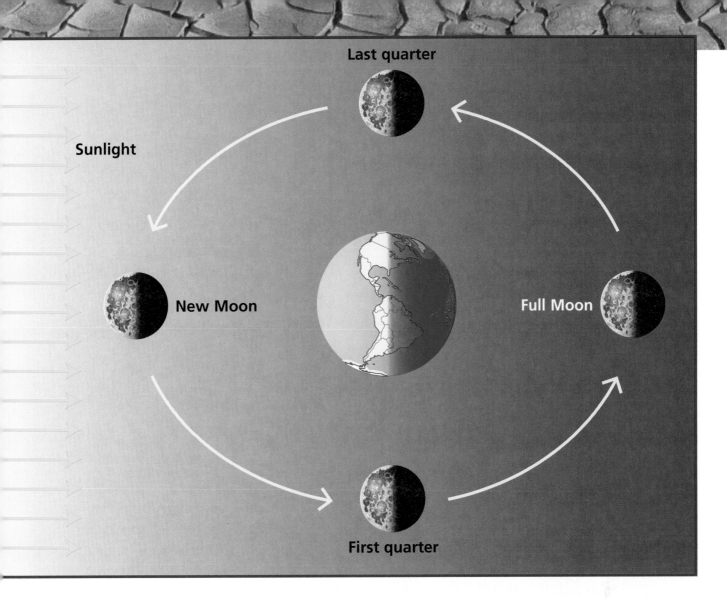

Last quarter

Sunlight

New Moon

Full Moon

First quarter

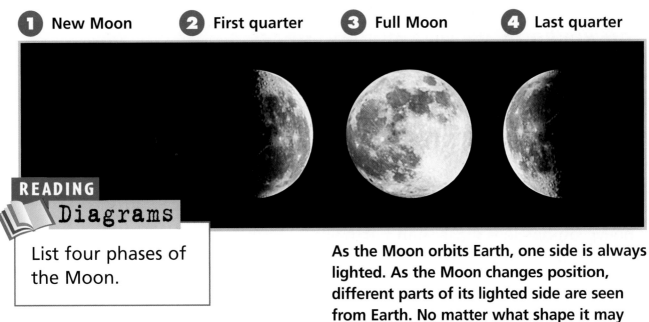

1 New Moon   **2** First quarter   **3** Full Moon   **4** Last quarter

READING
Diagrams

List four phases of
the Moon.

As the Moon orbits Earth, one side is always
lighted. As the Moon changes position,
different parts of its lighted side are seen
from Earth. No matter what shape it may
look like, the Moon is always a sphere.

The U.S. *Apollo 11* astronauts landed on the Moon on July 20, 1969.

How Are Earth and the Moon Different?

Both Earth and the Moon are spheres that rotate and revolve. They also receive light from the Sun. In most ways, however, Earth and the Moon are quite different. A day on Earth lasts 24 hours, while a day on the Moon lasts more than 27 Earth days.

The Moon is about one-fourth the size of Earth. The Moon has less mass than Earth. The Moon also has less gravity. The Moon's gravity is about one-sixth of Earth's gravity. If you weigh 30 kilograms (66 pounds) on Earth, you would weigh only 5 kilograms (11 pounds) on the Moon!

Craters (KRAY·tuhrz) cover most of the Moon's surface. A crater is a hollow area, or pit, in the ground. Some of the Moon's craters may have been formed by ancient volcanoes. Most, however, were caused by chunks of rock or metal from space that crashed into the Moon. Some of the Moon's craters are very large. Others are quite small.

Earth has few craters. Most objects from space burn up before they reach Earth. The air and water on Earth also cause craters here to erode, or wear away. The Moon has no air.

Water is found in many places on Earth. It is in the air. It is in oceans, rivers, lakes, and streams. Water is also found in the ground. The Moon has no liquid water. Water is needed by all living things. Because the Moon has no air or liquid water, there can be no life there. Astronauts were able to visit the Moon because their spacesuits provided air and protection.

READING **Cause and Effect**
What causes the craters on the Moon's surface?

Earth's surface is almost three-quarters water. There are few craters on Earth. Earth supports life.

Large and small craters cover the Moon's rocky surface. There is no liquid water on the Moon.

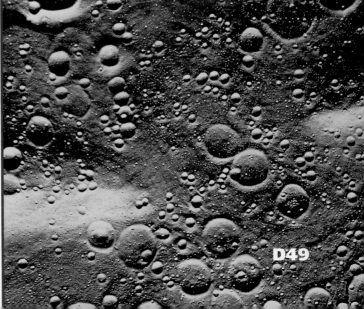

D49

Use Patterns

Rachel observed the Moon on different days during one month. She drew her observations on this calendar. There were some days she did not observe the Moon. Can you predict the shape of the Moon on the days she did not observe it?

Procedure

1. **Observe** Study the calendar shown here.

2. Look for similar shapes and patterns of the Moon.

Drawing Conclusions

1. **Predict** What do you think the Moon's shape was on Wednesday, January 9? Compare it with the shape of the Moon on January 8 and January 11. Draw your prediction.

2. **Predict** What was the Moon's shape on Friday, January 25? Compare it with the shape of the Moon on January 24 and January 26. Draw your prediction.

J A N U A R Y						
Sunday	Monday	Tuesday	Wednesday	Thursday	Friday	Saturday
		1	2	3	4	5
6	7	8	9	10	11	12
13	14	15	16	17	18	19
20	21	22	23	24	25	26
27	28	29	30	31		

3. **Predict** Draw the shape of the Moon you would expect to see on January 29. What helped you decide on that shape?

4. **Observe** Observe the change in the shape of the Moon in the sky for one month. Draw the shape in a calendar like the one shown above. Describe how the pattern changes.

Why It Matters

Earth provides you with things you need to survive, such as water, air, and temperatures that aren't too hot or too cold. The Moon is Earth's nearest neighbor in space. However, the Moon cannot support life. It is very hot in some places and very cold in others. The Moon doesn't have any air or liquid water.

e-Journal Visit our Web site www.science.mmhschool.com to do a research project on the Moon.

Think and Write

1. What shape is the Moon? Why does it appear to change shape?

2. Explain what the term "a phase of the Moon" means. Identify the four main phases.

3. Why does the Moon appear to shine?

4. **INQUIRY SKILL** **Predict** Last night it was a new Moon. What will the next main phase be?

5. **Critical Thinking** Why is there no life on the Moon?

L·I·N·K·S

MATH LINK

Use a calculator. How much would you weigh on the Moon? It's easy to figure out. Weigh yourself at home. Your weight will probably be in pounds. Divide your Earth weight by six to find your Moon weight. Use a calculator to help you.

LITERATURE LINK

Read Up, Up, and Away! to learn about Mae Jemison, the first African American woman to go into space. When you finish reading this book, imagine a day on the space shuttle. Try the activities at the end of the book.

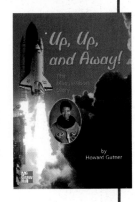

WRITING LINK

Writing a Story Write a science-fiction story about what it would be like to live on the Moon. Include characters, a setting, and a sequence of events with a problem that is solved at the end. Perform your story for an audience. Tape your story so you can watch it later.

TECHNOLOGY LINK

LOG ON Visit www.science.mmhschool.com for more links.

6

The Sun and Its Planets

Vocabulary

solar system, D54

planet, D54

star, D55

telescope, D58

lens, D58

Get Ready

When you look at the night sky, you see many different objects. You can see the Moon and the stars. You can also see some of Earth's other neighbors—planets. What do you see when you look up at the night sky?

Inquiry Skill

You **observe** when you use one or more of the senses to identify or learn about an object or event.

Explore Activity

How Do Planets Move?

Materials

sign for each planet

2 signs for the Sun

Procedure

1. **Make a Model** Take turns with other groups of classmates. Model the motion of the planets around the Sun. When you are not doing the modeling, make as many observations as you can.

2. **Observe** Listen to the student who is modeling Earth. He or she will describe what can be seen from Earth in the night sky.

Drawing Conclusions

1. What planets were visible from Earth the first time you modeled the motions of the planets? What planets were visible the second time?

2. How did Earth's motion affect what planets could be seen from Earth? How did the motion of the other planets affect what planets could be seen from Earth?

3. Why does the position of the planets in the night sky change?

4. **FURTHER INQUIRY** **Observe** How would the position of Venus change in your model if that classmate moved faster or slower around the Sun? Use the model to test your ideas.

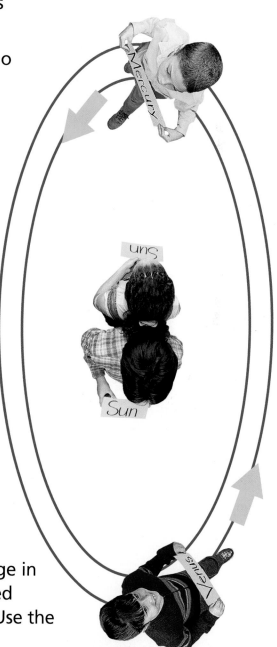

Read to Learn

Main Idea Our solar system includes the Sun, the nine planets, and their moons.

What Is the Solar System?

The Sun, Earth, and the Moon are part of a larger system called the **solar system**. The solar system is made up of the Sun and all the objects that orbit it.

Earth is one of nine **planets** (PLAN·itz) that orbit the Sun. A planet is a large body of rock or gas that orbits the Sun. Each planet is a different size. Some are smaller than Earth, and some are larger. Each planet rotates on its axis and revolves around the Sun as Earth does. Here is the order of the planets from the Sun: Mercury, Venus, Earth, Mars, Jupiter, Saturn, Uranus, Neptune, and Pluto. This sentence may help you remember the order: My Very Excellent Mother Just Served Us Nine Pizzas.

The Nine Planets Revolve Around the Sun

Sun

Mercury

Venus

Earth

Mars

The Sun is a **star**. A star is a hot, glowing ball of gases. The Sun is only a medium-sized star. It looks larger than any other star because it is the closest star to Earth.

The Sun is very big compared with Earth. It is so big that if it were hollow, more than one million Earths would fit inside it! The Sun looks small because it is very far from Earth. The Sun is so far away that it takes eight minutes for sunlight to make the trip to Earth.

Earth gets heat as well as light from the Sun. It's a good thing we live at this distance from the Sun. If we were much closer, Earth would be too hot to live on. If we were much farther away, Earth would be too cold for living things.

What is in our solar system?

Jupiter

Uranus

Pluto

Neptune

Saturn

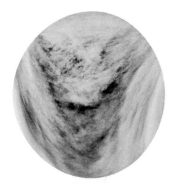

Mercury is the closest planet to the Sun. It looks a lot like Earth's Moon.

Space probes have visited cloud-covered **Venus** many times.

What Are the Nine Planets Like?

Like the Moon, planets have no light of their own. They reflect sunlight. Light reflected from the surface of the Moon and the planets shines steadily.

The name *planet* comes from a word meaning "wanderer." True to their name, planets appear to wander through the sky. Each planet moves in a different orbit and at a different speed. The planets are always moving and changing positions.

The planets are divided into two groups—the inner planets and the outer planets. The inner planets are the four planets closest to the Sun—Mercury, Venus, Earth, and Mars.

The inner planets are all small and made up of solid, rocklike materials.

Mars has some water, but most of it is frozen ice. Mars is known as the "red planet" because of its reddish rocks and soil.

Earth is our home. It is the only planet with liquid water.

Jupiter is the largest planet in our solar system. The Great Red Spot on Jupiter has been whirling around for 300 years.

Saturn is known for its thousands of beautiful rings. They are made up of different-sized bits of ice and rock that orbit the planet.

The outer planets are Jupiter, Saturn, Uranus, Neptune, and Pluto. All of the outer planets are made up mostly of gases, except for Pluto. Pluto is made up of a mixture of rocky materials and frozen gases. The outer planets are much colder than the inner planets. They are farther from the Sun.

Uranus is called the "sideways planet" because it rotates on its side.

READING **Cause and Effect**
What causes the outer planets to be colder than the inner planets?

Neptune is more than two billion miles from Earth. It has a Great Dark Spot similar to Jupiter's Great Red Spot.

Little is known about **Pluto** because it is so far away.

QUICK LAB

Make a Letter Larger

FOLDABLES Make a Trifold Book.
(See p. R42.) Mark the book as shown.

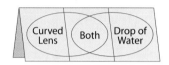

1. Cover a piece of newspaper with some wax paper.

2. **Observe** Put a small drop of water over a letter. How does it look?

3. **Experiment** Put water drops of different sizes over other letters. Observe.

4. How does the size of the drop affect the way the print looks?

5. **Infer** How is the curved lens in a telescope like the drop of water? Use the Venn Diagram on your Foldables book to record your answer.

The objects in our solar system are easier to see with a telescope.

How Do We Learn About Space?

The Sun, the Moon, and the planets are very far away. How do scientists learn about them? One tool they use is a **telescope** (TEL·uh·skohp). A telescope gathers light to make faraway objects appear larger, closer, and clearer. Telescopes gather light with mirrors and **lenses** (LENZ·uhz). A lens is a curved piece of glass.

▷ **What does a telescope do?**

Why It Matters

The solar system is Earth's "family" in space. Since early times people have wanted to know more about the other planets. Today telescopes and space probes give us a lot of important information. Do you like to look at the stars and planets at night? Now you know how to tell which objects are planets!

e-Journal Visit our Web site www.science.mmhschool.com to do a research project on the solar system.

Think and Write

1. What is the solar system?

2. What two things does Earth receive from the Sun?

3. How are the planets the same? How are they different?

4. How would life be different without the telescope?

5. **Critical Thinking** What if the outer planets were farther away from the Sun? How would this affect the planets' orbits around the Sun?

WRITING LINK

Personal Narrative Imagine yourself on a trip through space. What do you see as you pass by the planets? Write about an event that takes place. Use first-person point of view.

MATH LINK

Solve a problem. Jupiter has eight times as many moons as Mars. Mars has two moons. How many moons does Jupiter have? Explain how you found your answer.

LITERATURE LINK

Read *Mars Discovery* to learn about Mars. When you finish reading, make a list of the ways that Earth is similar to Mars. Try the activities at the end of the book.

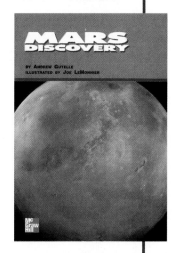

MARS DISCOVERY

BY ANDREW GUTELLE
ILLUSTRATED BY JOE LEMONNIER

TECHNOLOGY LINK

Science Newsroom CD-ROM Choose *Out for a Spin* to learn how Earth and Mars rotate and revolve.

 LOG ON Visit www.science.mmhschool.com for more links.

Chapter 8 Review

Vocabulary

Fill in each blank with the best word from the list.

axis, D37

crater, D49

orbit, D38

phase, D46

planet, D54

revolve, D38

rotate, D36

satellite, D46

star, D55

telescope, D58

1. Earth revolves or travels in a(n) _____ around the Sun.

2. A new Moon and a full Moon are two of the Moon's _____.

3. Mercury, Mars, and Earth are three of nine _____ in our solar system.

4. A tool that makes faraway objects seem closer is a(n) _____.

5. Anything that orbits another larger object in space is a(n) _____.

6. When a meteorite slams into the Moon, it makes a hollow area called a(n) _____.

7. Earth spins on an imaginary line called a(n) _____.

8. The Sun is a medium-sized _____.

Two ways Earth moves are that it:

9. _____

10. _____.

Test Prep

11. There are days and nights because _____.

    A the Sun rotates

    B the Moon rotates

    C Earth rotates

    D the Moon revolves around the Sun

12. Earth revolves around _____.

    F the equator

    G the poles

    H the Moon

    J the Sun

13. The apparent changes in the Moon's shape are the Moon's _____.

    A craters

    B phases

    C orbits

    D seasons

14. The two planets closest to Earth are _____.

    F Mars and Venus

    G Mars and Jupiter

    H Mars and the Moon

    J Venus and Mercury

15. The largest planet is _____.

    A Earth

    B Saturn

    C Jupiter

    D Mars

Concepts and Skills

16. **Reading in Science** Why does the Moon appear to change shape when viewed from Earth? Use the diagram below to help you answer the question.

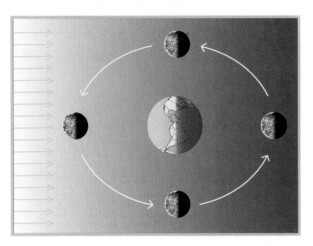

17. **Critical Thinking** Some places on Earth have 24 hours of daylight in the summer and 24 hours of darkness in the winter. Where are these places? Explain your answer.

18. **INQUIRY SKILL** **Predict** How would Earth's weather be different if Earth's axis was straight up and down, instead of tilted?

19. **Product Ads** Find ads for suntan lotion or sunscreen. Explain what the products claim to do. How do the ads try to interest people in the product?

20. **Scientific Methods** Scientists use tools to help them observe things. What tool has helped scientists to understand planets? How has it helped?

Did You Ever Wonder?

INQUIRY SKILL **Observe** You have learned about planets in our solar system. Explore the movement of a star or planet in the night sky. Explain what you see.

 LOG ON Visit **www.science.mmhschool.com** to boost your test scores.

Dr. Renée Roberta Fair
Meteorologist

In January 1999, tornadoes ripped through Little Rock, Arkansas. Eight people lost their lives. "It could have been much worse," says Renée Roberta Fair. She is a meteorologist at the Little Rock office of the National Oceanic and Atmospheric Administration (NOAA)—the U.S. weather agency. Thanks to her office, people were warned and took cover from the dangerous winds.

Fair's team uses radar and other high-tech tools to do their job. Instruments record important data, such as wind speed, wind direction, and rainfall. NOAA also uses the Internet to keep track of weather—and to let people know about weather conditions.

Studying weather is an important job. "Absolutely everything and everyone depends on weather—and weather information," says Fair. And we all depend on meteorologists to tell us what the weather's going to be!

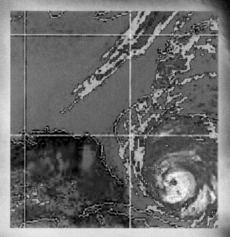

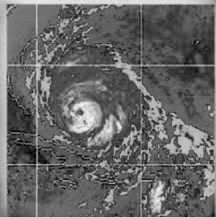

A hurricane roars toward the coast of Florida.

TOP 5 Most Expensive Hurricanes

Here's a list of the most expensive hurricanes in U.S. history. The costs are for rebuilding destroyed property.

1. Andrew, 1992: $26.5 billion
2. Hugo, 1989: $7 billion
3. Floyd, 1999: $4.5 billion
4. Fran, 1996: $3.2 billion
5. Opal, 1995: $3 billion

Write About It

1. Why is knowing about the weather important for everyone?
2. How did Dr. Fair and her team help save lives in 1999?

LOG ON Visit www.science.mmschool.com to learn more about meteorologists and weather prediction.

WATER CYCLE Story

Your goal is to write a story about the water cycle.

What to Do

Suppose you are a drop of water in a lake. What happens to you as you pass through each phase of the water cycle? How would you feel? Write a story about your adventures as a water drop.

Your story should explain the water cycle. Illustrate your pages with pictures and diagrams.

Moon Watch

Your goal is to make a chart. It will show how the Moon's position changes from day to day.

What to Do

Begin your observations when the Moon is crescent-shape. With a parent or guardian, look in the southwestern part of the sky just after sunset. Pick a point on the horizon directly under the Moon.

Hold your arm straight out and use your fist as a measuring tool. Measure how many fists above the horizon you see the Moon.

Record the Moon's position and elevation. Repeat the same measurements each day, at the same time, for one week.

Draw Conclusions

Describe the movement of the Moon in the sky over the week.

For Your Reference

Science Handbook

Health Handbook

Units of Measurement

Temperature

1. The temperature is 77 degrees Fahrenheit.

2. That is the same as 25 degrees Celsius.

3. Water boils at 212 degrees Fahrenheit.

4. Water freezes at 0 degrees Celsius.

Length and Area

1. This classroom is 10 meters wide and 20 meters long.

2. That means the area is 200 square meters.

2. 32 ounces is the same as 2 pounds.

3. The mass of the bat is 907 grams.

Mass and Weight

1. That baseball bat weighs 32 ounces.

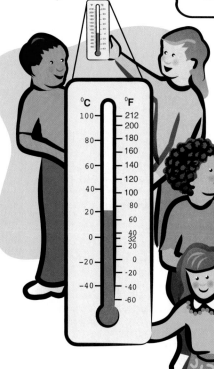

Measurement

Volume of Fluids

Weight/ Force

Rate

1. This bottle of juice has a volume of 1 liter.

2. That is a little more than 1 quart.

3. I weigh 85 pounds. That is a force of 380.8 newtons.

1. She can walk 20 meters in 5 seconds.

2. That means her speed is 4 meters per second.

Table of Measurements

SI (International System) of Units	English System of Units
Temperature Water freezes at 0 degrees Celsius (°C) and boils at 100°C.	**Temperature** Water freezes at 32 degrees Fahrenheit (°F) and boils at 212°F.
Length and Distance 10 millimeters (mm) = 1 centimeter (cm) 100 centimeters = 1 meter (m) 1,000 meters = 1 kilometer (km)	**Length and Distance** 12 inches (in.) = 1 foot (ft) 3 feet = 1 yard (yd) 5,280 feet = 1 mile (mi)
Volume 1 cubic centimeter (cm^3) = 1 milliliter (mL) 1,000 milliliters = 1 liter (L)	**Volume of Fluids** 8 fluid ounces (fl oz) = 1 cup (c) 2 cups = 1 pint (pt) 2 pints = 1 quart (qt) 4 quarts = 1 gallon (gal)
Mass 1,000 milligrams (mg) = 1 gram (g) 1,000 grams = 1 kilogram (kg)	**Weight** 16 ounces (oz) = 1 pound (lb) 2,000 pounds = 1 ton (T)
Area 1 square kilometer (km^2) = 1 km x 1 km 1 hectare = 10,000 square meters (m^2)	**Rate** mph = miles per hour
Rate m/s = meters per second km/h = kilometers per hour	
Force 1 newton (N) = 1 kg x 1m/s^2	

Use a Hand Lens

You use a hand lens to magnify an object, or make the object look larger. With a hand lens, you can see details that would be hard to see without the hand lens.

Magnify a Piece of Cereal

1. Place a piece of your favorite cereal on a flat surface. Look at the cereal carefully. Draw a picture of it.
2. Hold the hand lens so that it is just above the cereal. Look through the lens, and slowly move it away from the cereal. The cereal will look larger.

3. Keep moving the hand lens until the cereal begins to look blurry. Then move the lens a little closer to the cereal until you can see it clearly.
4. Draw a picture of the cereal as you see it through the hand lens. Fill in details that you did not see before.
5. Repeat this activity using objects you are studying in science. It might be a rock, some soil, a seed, or something else.

Use a Microscope

Hand lenses make objects look several times larger. A microscope, however, can magnify an object to look hundreds of times larger.

Examine Salt Grains

1. Place the microscope on a flat surface. Always carry a microscope with both hands. Hold the arm with one hand, and put your other hand beneath the base.
2. Look at the drawing to learn the different parts of the microscope.
3. Move the mirror so that it reflects light up toward the stage. Never point the mirror directly at the Sun or a bright light. Bright light can cause permanent eye damage.
4. Place a few grains of salt on the slide. Put the slide under the stage clips on the stage. Be sure that the salt grains are over the hole in the stage.
5. Look through the eyepiece. Turn the focusing knob slowly until the salt grains come into focus.
6. Draw what the grains look like through the microscope.
7. Look at other objects through the microscope. Try a piece of leaf, a strand of human hair, or a pencil mark.
8. Draw what each object looks like through the microscope. Do any of the objects look alike? If so, how? Are any of the objects alive? How do you know?

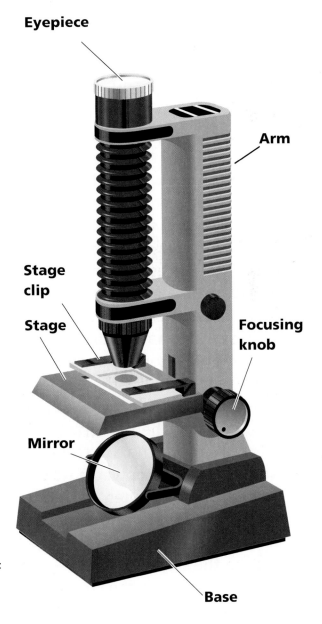

Eyepiece

Arm

Stage clip

Stage

Focusing knob

Mirror

Base

Measure Time

You use timing devices to measure how long something takes to happen. Some timing devices you use in science are a clock with a second hand and a stopwatch. Which one is more accurate?

Comparing a Clock and a Stopwatch

1. Look at a clock with a second hand. The second hand is the hand that you can see moving. It measures seconds.

2. Get an egg timer with falling sand. When the second hand of the clock points to 12, tell your partner to start the egg timer. Watch the clock while the sand in the egg timer is falling.

3. When the sand stops falling, count how many seconds it took. Record this measurement. Repeat the activity, and compare the two measurements.

4. Look at a stopwatch. Click the button on the top right. This starts the time. Click the button again. This stops the time. Click the button on the top left. This sets the stopwatch back to zero. Notice that the stopwatch tells time in hours, minutes, seconds, and hundredths of a second.

5. Repeat the activity in steps 1–3, but use the stopwatch instead of a clock. Make sure the stopwatch is set to zero. Click the top right button to start timing. Click the

button again when the sand stops falling. Make sure you and your partner time the sand twice.

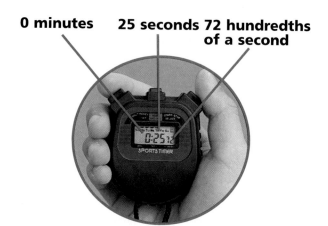

0 minutes   **25 seconds 72 hundredths of a second**

More About Time

1. Use the stopwatch to time how long it takes an ice cube to melt under cold running water. How long does an ice cube take to melt under warm running water?

2. Match each of these times with the action you think took that amount of time.

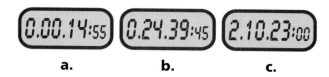

0.00.14:55	0.24.39:45	2.10.23:00
a.	b.	c.

1. A Little League baseball game
2. Saying the Pledge of Allegiance
3. Recess

Measure Length

You measure length to find out how long something is or how far away something is.

Find Length with a Ruler

1. Look at this section of a ruler. Each centimeter (cm) is divided into 10 millimeters (mm). How long is the paper clip?
2. The length of the paper clip is 3 centimeters plus 2 millimeters. You can write this length as 3.2 centimeters.
3. Place a ruler on your desk. Lay a pencil against the ruler so that one end of the pencil lines up with the left edge of the ruler. Record the length of the pencil.
4. Measure the length of another object. What unit of measure did you use?
5. Ask a partner to measure the same object. Compare your answers. Explain how measurements can be slightly different even if the item measured is the same.

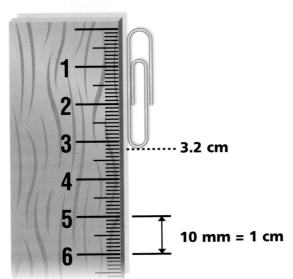

3.2 cm

10 mm = 1 cm

Measuring Area

Area is the amount of surface something covers. To find the area of a rectangle, multiply the rectangle's length by its width. For example, the rectangle here is 3 centimeters long and 2 centimeters wide. Its area is 3 cm x 2 cm = 6 square centimeters. You write the area as 6 cm^2.

1. Find the area of your science book. Measure the book's length to the nearest centimeter. Measure its width.
2. Multiply the book's length by its width. Remember to put the answer in cm^2.

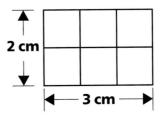

2 cm

3 cm

More About Length

Another tool that measures length is called a caliper. It measures distances and thicknesses. It has two movable, curved legs on a hinge. Try measuring a baseball with a caliper. How wide is it from one side to the other?

Measure Mass

Mass is the amount of matter an object has. You use a balance to measure mass. To find the mass of an object, you balance it with objects whose masses you know.

Measure the Mass of a Box of Crayons

1. Place the balance on a flat, level surface.
2. The pointer should point to the middle mark. If it does not, move the slider a little to the right or left to balance the pans.
3. Gently place a box of crayons on the left pan. Add gram masses to the right pan until the pans are balanced.
4. Count the numbers on the masses that are in the right pan. The total is the mass of the box of crayons, in grams.

5. Record this number. After the number, write a *g* for "grams."

More About Mass

What would happen if you replaced the crayons with a paper clip or a pineapple? You may not have enough masses to balance the pineapple. It has a mass of about 1,000 grams. That's the same as 1 kilogram, because *kilo* means "1,000." Measure other objects and record your measurements.

Measure Volume

Have you ever used a measuring cup? Measuring cups measure the volume of liquids. Volume is the amount of space something takes up. In science you use special measuring cups called beakers and graduated cylinders. These containers are marked in milliliters (mL).

Measure the Volume of a Liquid

1. Look at the beaker and at the graduated cylinder. The beaker has marks for each 25 mL up to 200 mL. The graduated cylinder has marks for each 1 mL up to 100 mL.

2. The surface of the water in the graduated cylinder curves up at the sides. You measure the volume by reading the height of the water at the flat part. What is the volume of water in the graduated cylinder? How much water is in the beaker?

3. Pour 50 mL of water from a pitcher into a graduated cylinder. The water should be at the 50-mL mark on the graduated cylinder. If you go over the mark, pour a little water back into the pitcher.

4. Pour the 50 mL of water into a beaker.

5. Repeat steps 3 and 4 using 30 mL, 45 mL, and 25 mL of water.

6. Measure the volume of water you have in the beaker. Do you have about the same amount of water as your classmates?

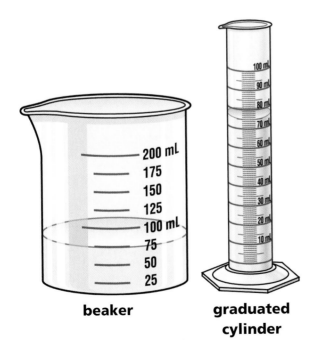

beaker   graduated cylinder

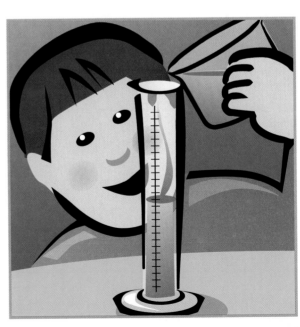

Measure Weight/Force

You use a spring scale to measure weight. An object has weight because the force of gravity pulls down on the object. Therefore, weight is a force. Like all forces, weight is measured in newtons (N).

Measure the Weight of an Object

1. Look at your spring scale to see how many newtons it measures. See how the measurements are divided. The spring scale shown here measures up to 10 N. It has a mark for every 1 N.

2. Hold the spring scale by the top loop. Put the object to be measured on the bottom hook. If the object will not stay on the hook, place it in a net bag. Then hang the bag from the hook.

3. Let go of the object slowly. It will pull down on a spring inside the scale. The spring is connected to a pointer. The pointer on the spring scale shown here is a small arrow.

4. Wait for the pointer to stop moving. Read the number of newtons next to the pointer. This is the object's weight. The mug in the picture weighs 3 N.

More About Spring Scales

You probably weigh yourself by standing on a bathroom scale. This is a spring scale. The force of your body stretches a spring inside the scale. The dial on the scale is probably marked in pounds—the English unit of weight. One pound is equal to about 4.5 newtons.

Here are some spring scales you may have seen.

Measure Temperature

Temperature is how hot or cold something is. You use a thermometer to measure temperature. A thermometer is made of a thin tube with colored liquid inside. When the liquid gets warmer, it expands and moves up the tube. When the liquid gets cooler, it contracts and moves down the tube. You may have seen most temperatures measured in degrees Fahrenheit (°F). Scientists measure temperature in degrees Celsius (°C).

Read a Thermometer

1. Look at the thermometer shown here. It has two scales—a Fahrenheit scale and a Celsius scale. Every 20 degrees on each scale has a number.

2. What is the temperature shown on the thermometer? At what temperature does water freeze? Give your answers in °F and in °C.

How Is Temperature Measured?

1. Fill a large beaker about one-half full of cool water. Hold the thermometer in the water by using a clamp. Do not let the thermometer bulb touch the beaker.

2. Wait until the liquid in the tube stops moving—about a minute. Read and record the temperature. Record the temperature scale you used.

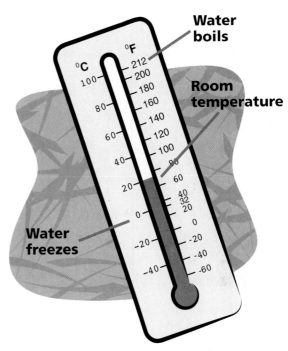

Water boils

Room temperature

Water freezes

3. Place the beaker with the thermometer on a hot plate and warm the beaker for two minutes. Be careful of the hot plate and warm water.

4. Record the temperature of the water. Use the same temperature scale you chose in Step 2.

Use Calculators: Add and Subtract

Sometimes after you make measurements, you have to add or subtract your numbers. A calculator helps you do this.

Add and Subtract Rainfall Amounts

The table shows the amount of rain that fell in a town each week during the summer.

Week	Rain (cm)
1	3
2	5
3	2
4	0
5	1
6	6
7	4
8	0
9	2
10	2
11	6
12	5

1. Make sure the calculator is on. Press the **ON** key.
2. To add the numbers, enter a number and press ⊕ . Repeat until you enter the last number. Then press ⊜ . You do not have to enter the zeros. Your total should be 36.

3. What if you found out that you made a mistake in your measurement? Week 1 should be 2 cm less, week 6 should be 3 cm less, week 11 should be 1 cm less, and week 12 should be 2 cm less. Subtract these numbers from your total. You should have 36 displayed on the calculator. Press ⊖ , and enter the first number you want to subtract. Repeat until you enter the last number. Then press ⊜ .

Use Technology

Use Calculators: Multiply and Divide

Sometimes after you make measurements, you have to multiply or divide your measurements to get other information. A calculator helps you multiply and divide, especially if the numbers have decimal points.

Multiply Decimals

What if you are measuring the width of your classroom? You discover that the floor is covered with tiles and the room is exactly 32 tiles wide. You measure a tile, and it is 22.7 centimeters wide. To find the width of the room, you can multiply 32 by 22.7.

1. Make sure the calculator is on. Press the **ON** key.
2. Press **3** and **2**.
3. Press **×**.
4. Press **2**, **2**, **.**, and **7**.
5. Press **=**. Your total should be 726.4. That is how wide the room is in centimeters.

Divide Decimals

Now what if you wanted to find out how many desks placed side by side would be needed to reach across the room? You measure one desk, and it is 60 centimeters wide. To find the number of desks needed, divide 726.4 by 60.

Remember that numbers have different values depending on what position they are in. A six in the ones place means six. In the tens place it means 60.

1. Turn the calculator on.
2. Press **7**, **2**, **6**, **.**, and **4**.
3. Press **÷**.
4. Press **6** and **0**.
5. Press **=**. Your total should be about 12.1. This means you can fit 12 desks across the room with a little space left over.

Suppose the room was 35 tiles wide. How wide would the room be? How many desks would fit across it?

Use Computers

A computer has many uses. The Internet connects your computer to many other computers around the world, so you can collect all kinds of information. You can use a computer to show this information and write reports. Best of all, you can use a computer to explore, discover, and learn.

You can also get information from CD-ROMs. They are computer disks that can hold large amounts of information. You can fit a whole encyclopedia on one CD-ROM.

Use Computers for a Project

Here's a project that uses computers. You can do the project in a group.

1. Use a collecting net to gather a soil sample from a brook or stream. Collect pebbles, sand, and small rocks. Keep any small plants also. Return any fish or other animals to the stream right away.

2. After the sample has dried, separate the items in the sample. Use a camera to photograph the soil, pebbles, small rocks, and plants.

3. Each group can use one of the photos to help them start their research. Try to find out what type of rocks or soil you collected.

4. Use the Internet for your research. Find a map and mark your area on it. Identify the type of soil. What types of plants grow well in that type of soil?

Local Soil Data

5. Find Web sites from an agency such as the Department of Environmental Protection. Contact the group. Ask questions about samples you collected.

6. Use CD-ROMS or other sources from the library to find out how the rocks and soil in your sample formed.

Use Technology

email: Dear Ms. Simpson, Thank you for helping with our project. How does the water in the stream help erode the rocks faster?

7. Keep the information you have gathered in a folder. Review it with your group and use it to write a group report about your soil sample.

8. Each group will present and read a different part of the report. Have an adult help you to record your reports on a video recorder. Show your photographs in the video and explain what each represents. If you'd like, use music or other sounds to accompany the voices on the video recorder.

9. Make a list of computer resources you used to make your report. List Web sites, CD-ROM titles, or other computer resources. Show or read the list at the end of your presentation.

10. Discuss how the computer helped each group to do their report. What problems did each group encounter using the computer? How were the problems solved?

Make Graphs to Organize Data

Graphs can help organize data. Graphs make it easy to spot trends and patterns. There are many kinds of graphs.

Bar Graphs

A bar graph uses bars to show information. For example, what if you are growing a plant? Every week you measure how high the plant has grown. Here is what you find.

Week	Height (cm)
1	1
2	3
3	6
4	10
5	17
6	20
7	22
8	23

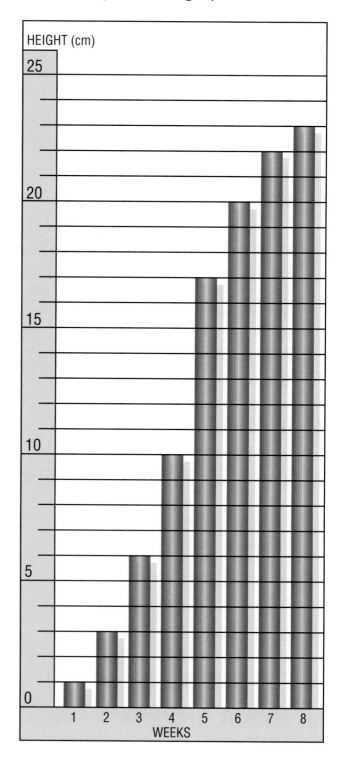

The bar graph at the right organizes the measurements so you can easily compare them.

1. Look at the bar for Week 2. Put your finger at the top of the bar. Move your finger straight over to the left to find how many centimeters the plant grew by the end of Week 2.

2. Between which two weeks did the plant grow most?

3. Look at the 0 on the graph. Is it just a label on a scale or does it have a meaning in the graph? Explain.

Represent Data

Pictographs

A pictograph uses symbols, or pictures, to show information. What if you collect information about how much water your family uses each day? Here is what you find.

Activity	Water Used Each Day (L)
Drinking	10
Showering	100
Bathing	120
Brushing teeth	40
Washing dishes	80
Washing hands	30
Washing clothes	160
Flushing toilet	50

You can organize this information into the pictograph shown here. In this pictograph each bottle means 20 liters of water. A half bottle means half of 20, or 10 liters of water.

1. Which activity uses the most water?
2. Which activity uses the least water?

Line Graphs

A line graph shows how information changes over time. What if you measure the temperature outdoors every hour starting at 6 A.M.? Here is what you find.

Time	Temperature (°C)
6 A.M.	10
7 A.M.	12
8 A.M.	14
9 A.M.	16
10 A.M.	18
11 A.M.	20

Now collect outside temperatures on your own each hour. Follow these steps to make a line graph.

1. Make a scale along the bottom and side of the graph as shown. Label the scales.
2. Plot points on the graph.
3. Connect the points with a line.
4. How do the temperatures and times relate to each other? Compare your graph to the one shown.

A Family's Daily Use of Water

Drinking

Showering

Bathing

Brushing teeth

Washing dishes

Washing hands

Washing clothes

Flushing toilet

= 20 liters of water

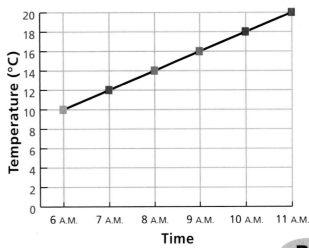

Make Maps, Tables, Charts

Locate Places

A map is a drawing that shows an area from above. Most maps have numbers and letters along the top and side. What if you wanted to find the library on the map below? It is located at D7. Place a finger on the letter D along the side of the map and another finger on the number 7 at the top. Then move your fingers straight across and down the map until they meet. The library is located where D and 7 meet.

1. What building is located at G3?
2. The hospital is located three blocks south and three blocks east of the library. What is its number and letter?
3. Make a map of an area in your community. It might be a park or the area between your home and school. Include numbers and letters along the top and side. Use a compass to find north, and mark north on your map. Exchange maps with classmates.

Idea Maps

The map below left shows how places are connected to each other. Idea maps, on the other hand, show how ideas are connected to each other. Idea maps help you organize information about a topic.

Look at the idea map below. It connects ideas about water. This map shows that Earth's water is either fresh water or salt water. The map also shows four sources of fresh water. You can see that there is no connection between "rivers" and "salt water" on the map. This reminds you that salt water does not flow in rivers.

Make an idea map about a topic you are learning in science. Your map can include words, phrases, or even sentences. Arrange your map in a way that makes sense to you and helps you understand the ideas.

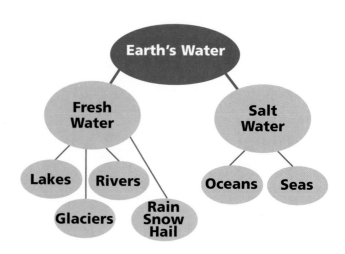

R 18

Make Tables and Charts to Organize Data

Tables help to organize data during experiments. Most tables have columns that run up and down, and rows that run across. The columns and rows have headings that tell you what kind of data goes in each part of the table.

A Sample Table

What if you are going to do an experiment to find out how long different kinds of seeds take to sprout? Before you begin the experiment, you should set up your table. Follow these steps.

1. In this experiment you will plant 20 radish seeds, 20 bean seeds, and 20 corn seeds. Your table must show how many of each kind of seed sprouted on days 1, 2, 3, 4, and 5.

2. Make your table with columns, rows, and headings. You might use a computer. Some computer programs let you build a table with just the click of a mouse. You can delete or add columns and rows if you need to.

3. Give your table a title. Your table could look like the one here.

Make a Table

Plant 20 bean seeds in each of two trays. Keep each tray at a different temperature and observe the trays for seven days. Make a table to record, examine, and evaluate the information of this experiment. How do the columns, rows, and headings of your table relate to one another?

Make a Chart

A chart is simply a table with pictures, as well as words to label the rows or columns. Make a chart that shows the information of the above experiment.

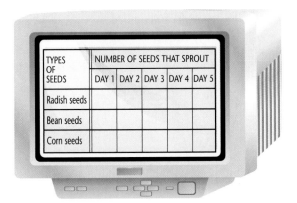

TYPES OF SEEDS	NUMBER OF SEEDS THAT SPROUT				
	DAY 1	DAY 2	DAY 3	DAY 4	DAY 5
Radish seeds					
Bean seeds					
Corn seeds					

The Skeletal System

The Skeleton

The skeleton is a system of the human body. It is the frame that supports the body. The skeleton is made up of bones and has several jobs.

- It gives the body its shape.
- It protects organs in the body.
- It works with muscles to move the body.

Each of the 206 bones of the skeleton is the size and shape best fitted to do its job. For example, long and strong leg bones support the body's weight. The skull protects the brain. The hip bone helps you move.

1. What is the skeleton?
2. Describe several jobs of bones.

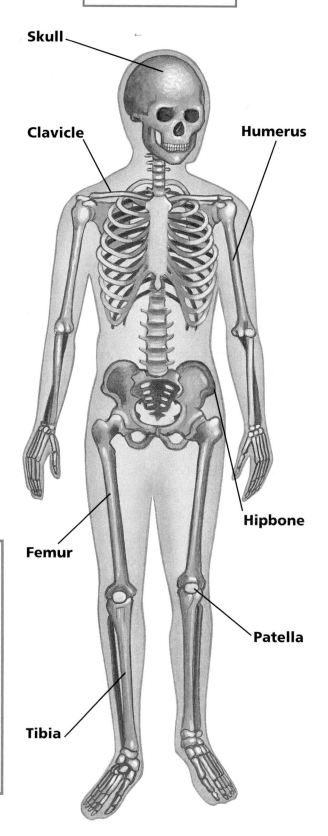

Skull

Clavicle

Humerus

Femur

Hipbone

Patella

Tibia

CARE!

- Exercise to keep your skeletal system in good shape.
- Don't overextend your joints.
- Eat foods rich in vitamins and minerals. Your bones need the minerals calcium and phosphorus to grow strong.

Bones

1. A bone is covered with a tough but thin membrane that has many small blood vessels. The blood vessels bring nutrients and oxygen to the living parts of the bone and remove wastes.

2. Inside some bones is a soft tissue known as marrow. Yellow marrow is made mostly of fat cells and is one of the body's energy reserves. It is usually found in the long, hollow spaces of long bones.

3. Part of the bone is compact, or solid. It is made up of living bone cells and non-living materials. The nonliving part is made up of layers of hardened minerals such as calcium and phosphorus. In between the mineral layers are living bone cells.

4. Red marrow fills the spaces in spongy bone. Red marrow makes new red blood cells, germ-fighting white blood cells, and cell fragments that stop a cut from bleeding.

5. Part of the bone is made of bone tissue that looks like a dry sponge. It is made of strong, hard tubes. It is also found in the middle of short, flat bones.

CARE!

- **Eat foods rich in vitamins and minerals. Your bones need the minerals calcium and phosphorus to grow strong.**
- **Be careful! Avoid sprains and fractures.**
- **Get help in case of injury.**

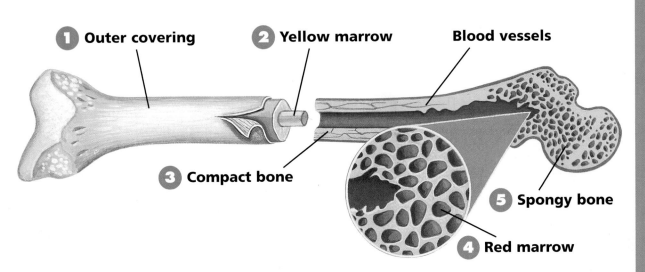

1 **Outer covering**   2 **Yellow marrow**   **Blood vessels**

3 **Compact bone**

5 **Spongy bone**

4 **Red marrow**

Joints

The skeleton has different types of joints. A joint is a place where two or more bones meet. Joints can be classified into three major groups—immovable joints, partly movable joints, and movable joints.

Types of Joints

IMMOVABLE JOINTS

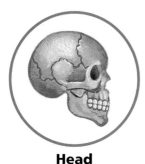

Head

Immovable joints are places where bones fit together too tightly to move. Nearly all the 29 bones in the skull meet at immovable joints. Only the lower jaw can move.

PARTLY MOVABLE JOINTS

Partly movable joints are places where bones can move only a little. Ribs are connected to the breastbone with these joints.

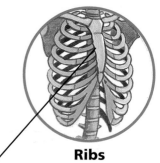

Breastbone

Ribs

MOVABLE JOINTS

Movable joints are places where bones can move easily. Use the information below to describe each type of movable joint. Explain how each type of joint allows movement.

Gliding joint

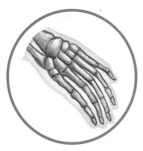

Hand and wrist

Small bones in the wrists and ankles meet at gliding joints. The bones can slide against one another. A gliding joint is similar to a sliding door. These joints allow some movement in all directions.

The hips are examples of ball-and-socket joints. The ball of one bone fits into the socket, or cup, of another bone. These joints allow bones to move back and forth, in a circle, and side to side.

Ball-and-socket joint

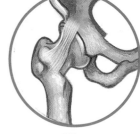

Hip

Hinge joint

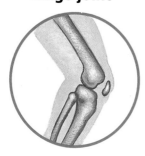

Knee

The knees are hinge joints. A hinge joint is similar to a door hinge. It allows bones to move back and forth in one direction.

The joint between the skull and neck is a pivot joint. It allows the head to move up and down, and side to side. A pivot joint is similar to a compass.

Pivot joint

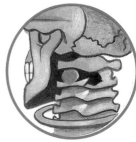

Neck

The Muscular System

1 A message from your brain causes this muscle, called the biceps, to contract. When a muscle contracts, it becomes shorter and thicker. As the biceps contracts, it pulls on the arm bone it is attached to.

2 Most muscles work in pairs to move bones. This muscle, called the triceps, relaxes when the biceps contracts. When a muscle relaxes, it becomes longer and thinner.

3 To straighten your arm, a message from your brain causes the triceps to contract. When the triceps contracts, it pulls on the bone it is attached to.

4 As the triceps contracts, the biceps relaxes. Your arm straightens.

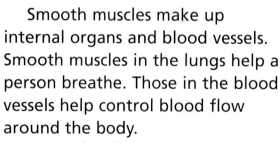

Three types of muscles make up the body—skeletal muscle, cardiac muscle, and smooth muscle.

The muscles that are attached to and move bones are called skeletal muscles. These muscles are attached to bones by a tough cord called a tendon. Skeletal muscles pull bones to move them. Muscles do not push bones.

Cardiac muscles are found in only one place in the body—the heart. The walls of the heart are made of strong cardiac muscles. When cardiac muscles contract, they squeeze blood out of the heart. When cardiac muscles relax, the heart fills with more blood.

Smooth muscles make up internal organs and blood vessels. Smooth muscles in the lungs help a person breathe. Those in the blood vessels help control blood flow around the body.

1. Name the three types of muscles.
2. Describe how muscles cause the body to move.

CARE!

- **Exercise to strengthen your muscles.**
- **Eat the right foods, and get plenty of rest.**

The Circulatory System

The circulatory system consists of the heart, blood vessels, and blood. Circulation is the flow of blood through the body. Blood is a liquid that contains red blood cells, white blood cells, and platelets. Red blood cells carry oxygen and nutrients to cells. White blood cells work to fight germs that enter the body. Platelets are cell fragments that make the blood clot.

The heart is a muscular organ about the size of a fist. It beats about 70 to 90 times a minute, pumping blood through the blood vessels. Arteries carry blood away from the heart. Some arteries carry blood to the lungs, where the cells pick up oxygen. Other arteries carry oxygen-rich blood from the lungs to all other parts of the body. Veins carry blood from other parts of the body back to the heart. Blood in most veins carries the wastes released by cells and has little oxygen. Blood flows from arteries to veins through narrow vessels called capillaries.

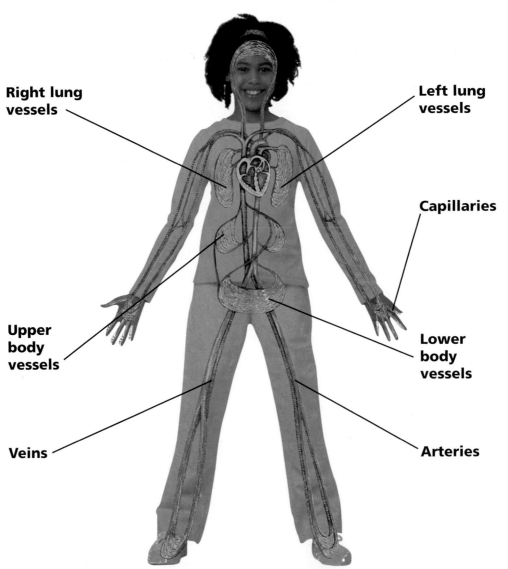

Right lung vessels

Left lung vessels

Capillaries

Upper body vessels

Lower body vessels

Veins

Arteries

The Heart

The heart has two sides, right and left, separated by a thick muscular wall. Each side has two chambers for blood. The upper chamber is the atrium. The lower chamber is the ventricle. Blood enters the heart through the vena cava. It leaves the heart through the aorta.

The pulmonary artery carries blood from the body into the lungs. Here carbon dioxide leaves the blood to be exhaled by the lungs. Fresh oxygen enters the blood to be carried to every cell in the body. Blood returns from the lungs to the heart through the pulmonary veins.

CARE!

- Don't smoke. The nicotine in tobacco makes the heart beat faster and work harder to pump blood.
- Never take illegal drugs, such as cocaine or heroin. They can damage the heart and cause heart failure.

How the Heart Works

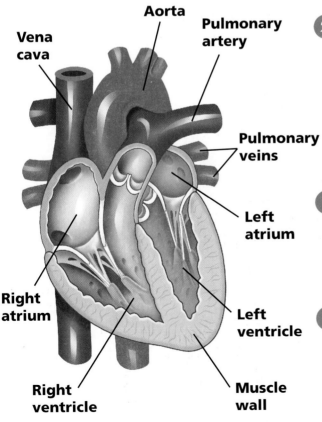

Vena cava
Aorta
Pulmonary artery
Pulmonary veins
Left atrium
Left ventricle
Muscle wall
Right ventricle
Right atrium

To the Lungs

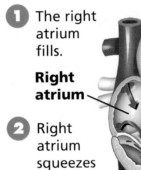

1 The right atrium fills.

Right atrium

2 Right atrium squeezes blood into right ventricle.

3 Right ventricle squeezes blood into pulmonary artery.

One-way valve

Right ventricle

From the Lungs

1 The left atrium fills.

2 Left atrium squeezes blood into left ventricle.

3 Left ventricle squeezes blood into aorta.

Left atrium

One-way valve

Left ventricle

R 25

The Respiratory System

The process of getting and using oxygen in the body is called respiration. When a person inhales, air is pulled into the nose or mouth. The air travels down into the trachea. In the chest the trachea divides into two bronchial tubes. One bronchial tube enters each lung. Each bronchial tube branches into smaller tubes called bronchioles.

At the end of each bronchiole are tiny air sacs called alveoli. The alveoli exchange carbon dioxide for oxygen.

Oxygen comes from the air we breathe. The main muscle that controls breathing is a dome-shaped sheet of muscle called the diaphragm.

To inhale, the diaphragm contracts and pulls down. To exhale, the diaphragm relaxes and returns to its dome shape.

CARE!

- **Don't smoke. Smoking damages your respiratory system.**

- **Exercise to strengthen your breathing muscles.**

- **If you ever have trouble breathing, tell an adult at once.**

Air Flow

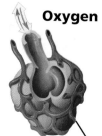

Carbon dioxide   **Oxygen**

Carbon dioxide diffuses into the alveoli. From there it is exhaled.

Capillary net

Alveoli

Fresh oxygen diffuses from the alveoli to the blood.

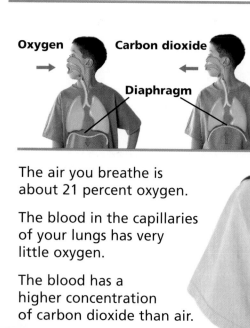

Oxygen →   Carbon dioxide ←

Diaphragm

The air you breathe is about 21 percent oxygen.

The blood in the capillaries of your lungs has very little oxygen.

The blood has a higher concentration of carbon dioxide than air.

Throat

Trachea

Lungs

Activity Pyramid

Physical fitness is the condition in which the body is healthy and works the best it can. The activity pyramid shows you the kinds of activities you should be doing to make your body more physically fit.

3–5 times a week Aerobic activities such as swimming, biking, climbing; sports activities such as basketball, handball

Occasionally
Inactive pastimes such as watching TV, playing board games, talking on the phone

2–3 times a week
Leisure activities such as gardening, golf, softball

Eating a variety of healthful foods and getting enough exercise and rest help people to stay healthy.

As people grow, the amounts and kinds of food and exercise the body needs may change.

Food Guide Pyramid

To make sure the body stays fit and healthy, a person needs to eat a balanced diet. The Food Guide Pyramid shows how many servings of each group a person should eat every day. Food provides energy and material for growth and repair of body parts. Vitamins and minerals keep the body healthy.

CARE!

- **Stay active every day.**
- **Eat a balanced diet.**
- **Drink plenty of water— 6 to 8 large glasses a day.**

Milk, yogurt, and cheese group
2–3 servings

Fats, oils, and sweets
Use sparingly

Meat, dry beans, eggs, and nuts group
2–3 servings

Vegetable group
3–5 servings

Fruit group
2–4 servings

Bread, cereal, rice, and pasta group
6–11 servings

The Digestive System

Digestion is the process of breaking down food into simple substances the body can use. Digestion begins when a person chews food. Chewing breaks the food down into smaller pieces and moistens it with saliva.

Digested food is absorbed in the small intestine. The walls of the small intestine are lined with villi. Villi are tiny fingerlike projections that absorb digested food. From the villi the blood transports nutrients to every part of the body.

It is important to eat healthful foods. Avoid eating foods with caffeine, sugar, and fat as these foods often lack the nutrients the body needs. Stay away from alcohol and drugs as these substances damage the body.

CARE!

- Chew your food well.
- Drink plenty of water to help move food through your digestive system.

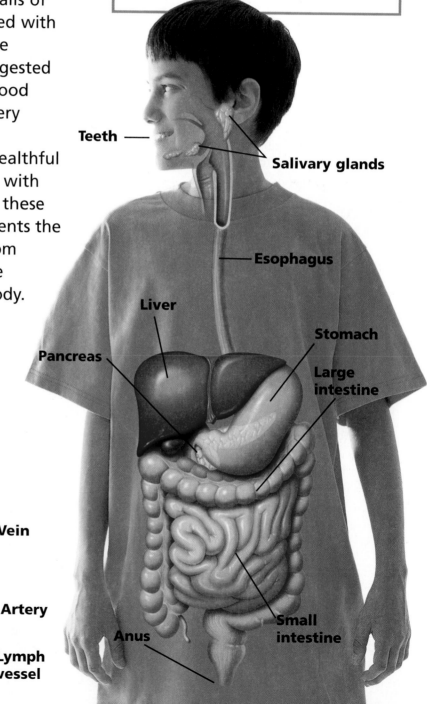

Teeth

Salivary glands

Esophagus

Liver

Stomach

Pancreas

Large intestine

Small intestine

Anus

Capillary

Villi

Vein

Artery

Lymph vessel

The Excretory System

Excretion is the process of removing waste products from the body. The liver filters wastes from the blood and converts them into urea. Urea is then carried to the kidneys for excretion.

The skin takes part in excretion when a person sweats. Glands in the inner layer of the skin produce sweat. Sweat is mostly water. Sweat tastes salty because it contains mineral salts the body doesn't need. There is also a tiny amount of urea in sweat.

Sweat is excreted onto the outer layer of the skin. Evaporation into the air takes place in part because of body heat. When sweat evaporates, a person feels cooler.

How You Sweat

Glands under your skin push sweat up to the surface, where it collects.

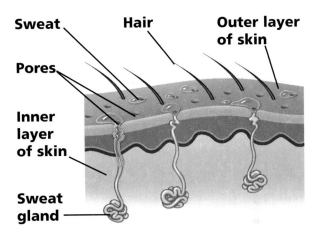

Sweat · Hair · Outer layer of skin · Pores · Inner layer of skin · Sweat gland

CARE!

● **Wash regularly to avoid body odor, clogged pores, and skin irritation.**

How Your Kidneys Work

1 Blood enters the kidney through an artery and flows into capillaries.

2 Sugars, salts, water, urea, and other wastes move from the capillaries to tiny nephrons.

3 Nutrients return to the blood and flow back out through veins.

4 Urea and other wastes become urine, which flows down the ureters.

5 Urine is stored in the bladder and excreted through the urethra.

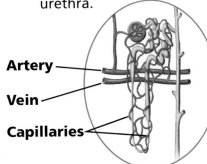

Artery · Vein · Capillaries

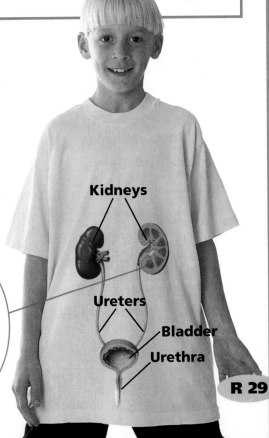

Kidneys · Ureters · Bladder · Urethra

The Nervous System

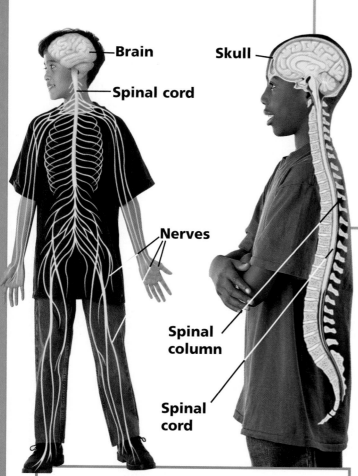
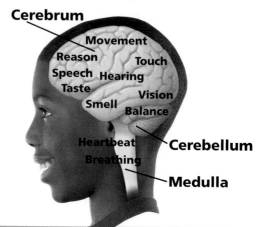

Brain

Spinal cord

Skull

Nerves

Spinal column

Spinal cord

Cerebrum

Movement

Reason

Touch

Speech Hearing

Taste

Vision

Smell

Balance

Heartbeat

Breathing

Cerebellum

Medulla

The nervous system has two parts. The brain and the spinal cord are the central nervous system. All other nerves are the outer nervous system.

The largest part of the brain is the cerebrum. A deep groove separates the right half, or hemisphere, of the cerebrum from the left half. Both sides of the cerebrum contain control centers for the senses.

The cerebellum lies below the cerebrum. It coordinates the skeletal muscles. It also helps in keeping balance.

The brain stem connects to the spinal cord. The lowest part of the brain stem is the medulla. It controls heartbeat, breathing, blood pressure, and the muscles in the digestive system.

CARE!

- To protect the brain and spinal cord, wear protective headgear when you play sports or exercise.

- Stay away from alcohol, which is a depressant and slows down the nervous system.

- Stay away from drugs, such as stimulants, which can speed up the nervous system.

The Endocrine System

Hormones are chemicals that control body functions. A gland that produces hormones is called an endocrine gland. Sweat from sweat glands flows out of tubes called ducts. Endocrine glands have no ducts.

The endocrine glands are scattered around the body. Each gland makes one or more hormones. Every hormone seeks out a target organ. This is the place in the body where the hormone acts.

Some Glands in the Endocrine System

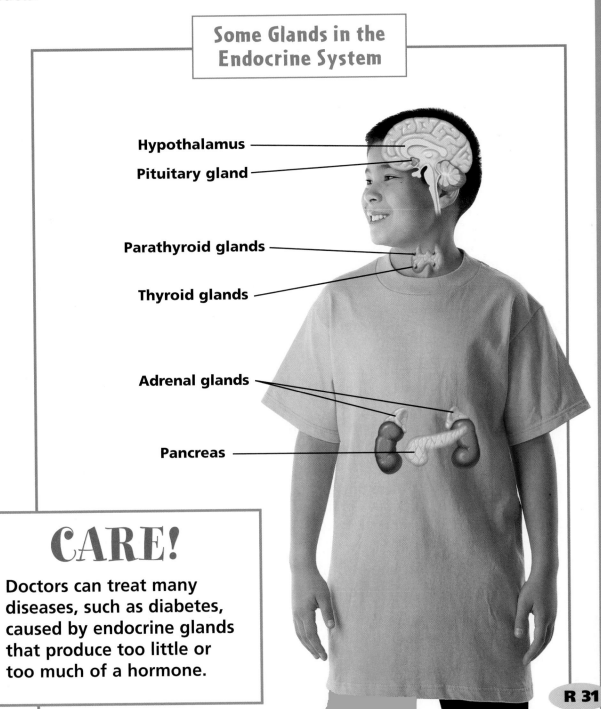

Hypothalamus

Pituitary gland

Parathyroid glands

Thyroid glands

Adrenal glands

Pancreas

CARE!

- Doctors can treat many diseases, such as diabetes, caused by endocrine glands that produce too little or too much of a hormone.

The Senses

Seeing

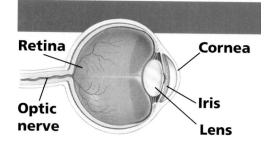

Retina **Cornea** **Optic nerve** **Iris** **Lens**

Light reflected from an object enters the eye and falls on the retina. Receptor cells change the light into electrical signals, or impulses. These impulses travel along the optic nerve to the vision center of the brain.

1 Light reflects off the tree and into your eyes.

2 The light passes through your cornea and the pupil in your iris.

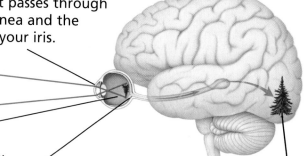

3 Your eye bends the light so it hits your retina.

4 Receptor cells on your retina change the light into electrical signals.

5 The impulses travel along neurons in your optic nerve to the seeing center of your brain.

Hearing

Hammer **Auditory nerve** **Hearing center**

1 Your outer ear collects sound waves.

2 They are funneled down your ear canal.

Eardrum **Anvil**

3 The eardrum vibrates.

Stirrup

4 Three tiny ear bones vibrate.

5 The cochlea vibrates.

Cochlea

6 Receptor cells inside your cochlea change.

7 The impulses travel along your auditory nerve to the brain's hearing center.

Sound waves enter the ear and cause the eardrum to vibrate. Receptor cells in the ear change the sound waves into impulses that travel along the auditory nerve to the hearing center of the brain.

CARE!

- Avoid loud music.
- Don't sit too close to the TV screen.

The Senses

Smelling

The sense of smell is really the ability to detect chemicals in the air. When a person breathes, chemicals dissolve in mucus in the upper part of the nose. When the chemicals come in contact with receptor cells, the cells send impulses along the olfactory nerve to the smelling center of the brain.

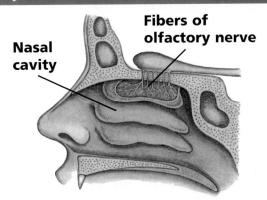

Nasal cavity

Fibers of olfactory nerve

Tasting

When a person eats, chemicals in food dissolve in saliva. Inside each taste bud are receptors that can sense the four main tastes—sweet, sour, salty, and bitter. The receptors send impulses along a nerve to the taste center of the brain. The brain identifies the taste of the food.

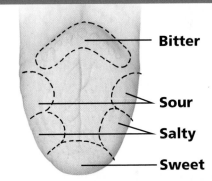

Bitter

Sour

Salty

Sweet

Touching

Receptor cells in the skin help a person tell hot from cold, wet from dry, and the light touch of a feather from the pressure of stepping on a stone. Each receptor cell sends impulses along sensory nerves to the spinal cord. The spinal cord then sends the impulses to the touch center of the brain.

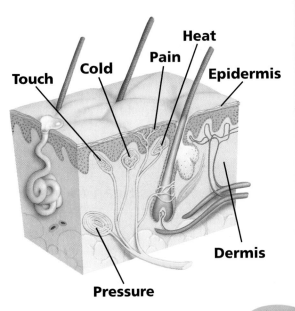

Touch Cold Pain Heat Epidermis

Dermis

Pressure

CARE!

● To prevent the spread of germs, always cover your mouth and nose when you cough or sneeze.

The Immune System

The immune system helps the body fight germs. Germs are tiny living things. The body is able to keep out harmful germs most of the time. Tears, saliva, and skin all help the body keep germs out. Sometimes germs get into the body. Usually white blood cells kill the germs before they can do any harm.

There are white blood cells in the blood vessels and in the lymph vessels. Lymph vessels are similar to blood vessels. Instead of blood, they carry lymph. Lymph nodes filter out harmful materials in the body. They also produce white blood cells to fight germs.

The white blood cells don't always get rid of the germs. Sometimes germs stay in the body and make it sick. When germs make the body sick, it is important to rest, eat healthful foods, and drink lots of water.

Lymph vessels run through your body to collect fluid and return it to the bloodstream.

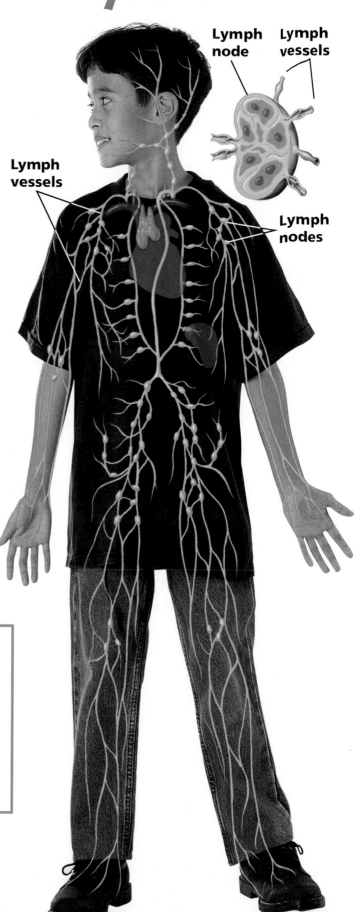

Lymph node

Lymph vessels

Lymph vessels

Lymph nodes

CARE!

- Be sure to get immunized against common diseases.
- Keep cuts clean to prevent infection.

Nutrients

Nutrients are materials in foods that your body uses to grow and stay healthy. Without nutrients you could not grow, move, think, or even live. Most foods that provide you with nutrients come from plants and animals.

There are six kinds of nutrients and each helps your body in a different way. Some help you grow. Others help repair damaged tissues in your body. Some help your body function properly. Still others give you energy. The six kinds of nutrients found in foods are carbohydrates, vitamins, minerals, proteins, fats, and water. A balance of different foods will give your body the nutrients that it needs.

Carbohydrates

Your body needs a constant supply of energy to keep working. **Carbohydrates** are a main source of energy for your body. There are two kinds of carbohydrates. One is *starch* and the other is *sugar*.

Starches provide long-lasting energy. Your body is able to store energy from starches longer than many other nutrients. Foods with starches are rice, potatoes, bread, cereal, and pasta.

It is easy to see what starch looks like.

1. Cut a raw potato into several pieces on a chopping board. Be careful with the knife.
2. Look for a whitish, milky liquid on the potato and on the knife. That liquid contains starch.
3. Check other foods for starch, such as cooked pasta or cooked rice.

Energy from sugars doesn't last as long as energy from starches. Fruits such as apples and oranges are made of sugars.

How can you test a food to tell if it is made of sugars? One way is to test them for a chemical reaction.

Finding Sugar

1. Label each of five small paper cups *apple juice*, *orange juice*, *olive oil*, *milk*, and *water*. Pour a small amount of each liquid into its labeled cup.
2. Your teacher will give you one glucose strip for each cup. Do not touch the strips with your fingers. Use a tweezer to hold a glucose strip in each liquid for two seconds.
3. What happened to each of the test strips? Record your observations in a chart.

If the food you tested contains sugar, the yellow test strip will turn green. Which foods tested contained sugar?

Vitamins and Minerals

Vitamins keep your body tissues healthy and protect you from illness. They are found in foods that come from plants and animals.

Very small amounts of vitamins are present in many foods. But this is all our bodies need to grow and stay healthy. These are some common vitamins you can find in foods.

Minerals come from Earth. They are found in small amounts in foods that come from plants and animals. Minerals help your blood, muscles, and nervous system. They help your bones to grow and function.

Calcium is a mineral that builds strong teeth and bones. It's found in foods such as yogurt, milk, cheese, and green vegetables. *Iron* helps red blood cells. It can be found in meat, beans, fish, and whole grains. Your body uses *zinc* to grow and to heal wounds. It is found in meat, fish, and eggs.

Vitamin	Sources	Benefits
A	Milk, fruit, carrots, green vegetables	Keeps eyes, teeth, gums, skin and hair healthy
C	Citrus fruits, strawberries, tomatoes	Helps heart, cells, and muscle function
D	Milk, fish, eggs	Helps keep teeth and bones strong

Protein and Water

Two of the most important nutrients for any living thing are **protein** and water. Proteins are part of every living cell. They are needed by all organisms. They help your body grow and help repair body cells. Foods such as milk, dairy products, meats, fish, and nuts are good sources of protein.

You can see the protein in some foods. Have you ever cooked an egg in a frying pan? An egg is rich in protein. Even the colorless part of the egg is made of protein. As the egg cooks, you can see the protein in this part of the egg become white.

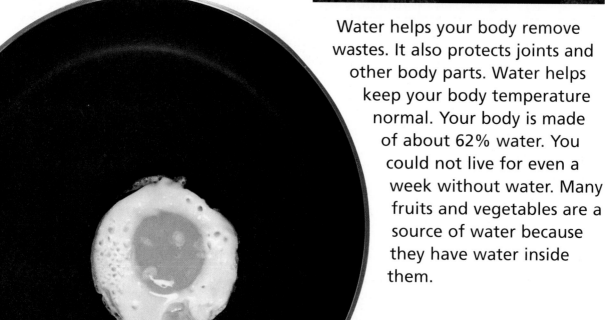

Water helps your body remove wastes. It also protects joints and other body parts. Water helps keep your body temperature normal. Your body is made of about 62% water. You could not live for even a week without water. Many fruits and vegetables are a source of water because they have water inside them.

Fats and Oils

Fats help your body to use other nutrients and to store vitamins. Fats keep your body warm and help brain cells and other body tissues work. Fats are found in meats, eggs, milk, butter, and nuts. Oils, such as those used in cooking, also contain fat.

While fat is needed for your body to work properly, it is needed only in small amounts. Some foods contain more fat than others.

Fat Check

POTATO CHIP

COOKIE

CARROT

APPLE

Here's a way to find out which foods contain a lot of fats.

1. Gather various foods, such as a potato chip, cookie, carrot, and apple.
2. Cut a brown paper bag into 3-inch (7-cm) squares. Label each square with the name of one of the foods.
3. Rub some of each food on the square. Let the square dry.
4. Hold each square up to the light. What effect do the different foods have on the paper?

Foods that leave a greasy mark or stain on the paper contain a lot of fat, or oils. Too much fat in our bodies can cause health problems.

Calories

The chemical energy in foods is measured in a unit called a **calorie**. You take calories of food energy into your body by eating. Then you use, or burn, calories with everything you do. Breathing, eating, digesting food, walking, even doing your homework uses calories.

You can compare the chemical energy from different foods. Most food packages contain a label that gives information about the food's nutrients.

Nutrition Facts
Serving Size 7 Crackers (31g)
Servings Per Container About 9

Amount Per Serving

Calories 140   Calories from Fat 45

	% Daily Value*
Total Fat 5g	8%
Saturated Fat 1g	5%
Polyunsaturated Fat 0g	
Monounsaturated Fat 1.5g	
Cholesterol 0mg	0%
Sodium 200mg	8%
Total Carbohydrate 21g	7%
Dietary Fiber 4g	14%
Sugars 0g	
Protein 3g	

Vitamin A 0%	•	Vitamin C 0%
Calcium 0%	•	Iron 8%

* Percent Daily Values are based on a 2,000 calorie diet. Your daily values may be higher or lower depending on your calorie needs:

	Calories:	2,000	2,500
Total Fat	Less than	65g	80g
Sat Fat	Less than	20g	25g
Cholesterol	Less than	300mg	300mg
Sodium	Less than	2,400mg	2,400mg
Total Carbohydrate		300g	375g
Dietary Fiber		25g	30g

Nutrition Facts
Serving Size 9 Crackers (31g)
Servings Per Container About 13

Amount Per Serving

Calories 120   Calories from Fat 15

	% Daily Value*
Total Fat 1.5g	2%
Saturated Fat .5g	3%
Cholesterol 0mg	0%
Sodium 210mg	9%
Total Carbohydrate 25g	8%
Dietary Fiber 1g	4%
Sugars 0g	
Protein 2g	

Vitamin A 0%	•	Vitamin C 0%
Calcium 0%	•	Iron 6%

* Percent Daily Values are based on a 2,000 calorie diet. Your daily values may be higher or lower depending on your calorie needs:

	Calories:	2,000	2,500
Total Fat	Less than	65g	80g
Sat Fat	Less than	20g	25g
Cholesterol	Less than	300mg	300mg
Sodium	Less than	2,400mg	2,400mg
Total Carbohydrate		300g	375g
Dietary Fiber		25g	30g

Calorie Comparison

Compare the calories on the food labels of these two boxes of crackers.

1. Look at the serving size on both labels. How many grams (g) of crackers are in a serving of each? Are they equal?
2. Compare the calories listed on the labels.
3. Which cracker provides more chemical energy per serving? Which cracker contains more sugar?
4. Now compare labels on two different types of foods, such as cheese and butter. Be sure the serving sizes are equal before comparing calories.

FOLDABLES™

by Dinah Zike

Folding Instructions

So how do you make a Foldables data organizer? The following pages offer step-by-step instructions—where and when to fold, where to cut—for making 11 basic Foldables data organizers. The instructions begin with the basic shapes, such as the hot dog fold, that were introduced on page xv.

Half-Book

Fold a sheet of paper ($8\frac{1}{2}$" x 11") in half.

1. This book can be folded vertically like a hot dog or …

2. … it can be folded horizontally like a hamburger.

Folded Book

1. Make a Half-Book.

2. Fold in half again like a hamburger.

This makes a ready-made cover and two small pages inside for recording information.

Two-Tab Book

Take a Folded Book and cut up the valley of the inside fold toward the mountain top.

This cut forms two large tabs that can be used front and back for writing and illustrations.

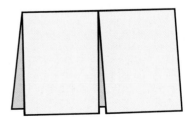

Pocket Book

1. Fold a sheet of paper ($8\frac{1}{2}$" x 11") in half like a hamburger.

2. Open the folded paper and fold one of the long sides up two inches to form a pocket. Refold along the hamburger fold so that the newly formed pockets are on the inside.

3. Glue the outer edges of the two-inch fold with a small amount of glue.

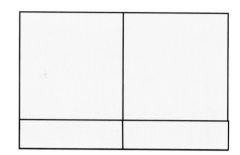

Shutter Fold

1. Begin as if you were going to make a hamburger, but instead of creasing the paper, pinch it to show the midpoint.

2. Fold the outer edges of the paper to meet at the pinch, or midpoint, forming a Shutter Fold.

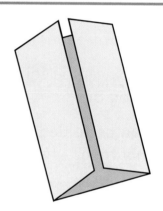

Trifold Book

1. Fold a sheet of paper ($8\frac{1}{2}$" x 11") into thirds.

2. Use this book as is, or cut into shapes.

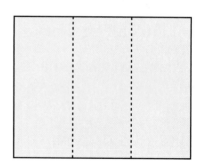

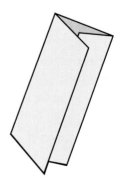

Three-Tab Book

1. Fold a sheet of paper like a hot dog.

2. With the paper horizontal and the fold of the hot dog up, fold the right side toward the center, trying to cover one half of the paper.

3. Fold the left side over the right side to make a book with three folds.

4. Open the folded book. Place one hand between the two thicknesses of paper and cut up the two valleys on one side only. This will create three tabs.

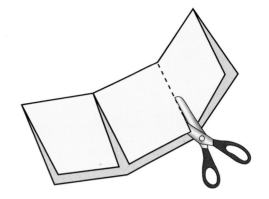

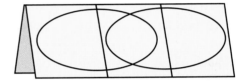

Layered-Look Book

1. Stack two sheets of paper ($8\frac{1}{2}$" x 11") so that the back sheet is one inch higher than the front sheet.

2. Bring the bottoms of both sheets upward and align the edges so that all of the layers or tabs are the same distance apart.

3. When all the tabs are an equal distance apart, fold the papers and crease well.

4. Open the papers and glue them together along the valley, or inner center fold, or staple them along the mountain.

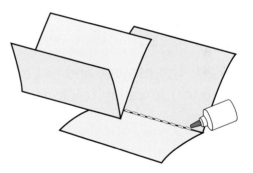

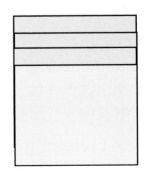

Four-Tab Book

1. Fold a sheet of paper ($8\frac{1}{2}$" x 11") in half like a hot dog.

2. Fold this long rectangle in half like a hamburger.

3. Fold both ends back to touch the mountain top or fold it like an accordion.

4. On the side with two valleys and one mountain top, make vertical cuts through one thickness of paper, forming four tabs.

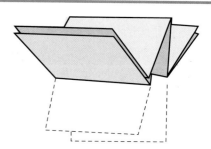

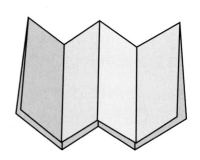

Four-Door Book

1. Make a Shutter Fold using 11" x 17" or 12" x 18" paper.

2. Fold the Shutter Fold in half like a hamburger. Crease well.

3. Open the project and cut along the two inside valley folds.

These cuts will form four doors on the inside of the project.

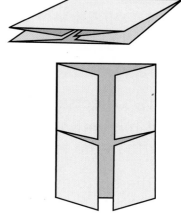

Folded Table or Chart

1. Fold the number of vertical columns needed to make the table or chart.

2. Fold the horizontal rows needed to make the table or chart.

3. Label the rows and columns.

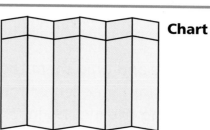

Chart

Table

Glossary

This Glossary will help you to pronounce and understand the meanings of the Science Words introduced in this book. The page number at the end of the definition tells where the word appears.

A

adaptation (ad′əp tā′shən) A special characteristic that helps an organism survive. (p. B50)

air (âr) A mixture of gases and dust. (p. D6)

air pressure (âr presh′ər) The force of air pushing down on Earth. (p. D9)

algae (al′jē) *pl. n., sing.* (-gə) Tiny one-celled organisms. (pp. B9, B27)

amber (am′bər) Hardened tree sap, often a source of insect fossils. (p. C22)

amphibian (am fib′ē ən) An animal that spends part of its life in water and part of its life on land. (p. A72)

anemometer (an′ə mom′i tər) A device that measures wind speed. (p. D25)

aqueduct (ak′wə dukt′) A pipe or channel for carrying water over long distances. (p. C32)

atmosphere (at′məs fîr′) Gases that surround Earth. (p. D6)

atom (at′əm) The smallest particle of matter. (p. F28)

axis (ak′sis) A real or imaginary line through the center of a spinning object. (p. D37)

PRONUNCIATION KEY

The following symbols are used throughout the Macmillan McGraw-Hill Science Glossaries.

a	at	e	end	o	hot	u	up	hw **white**	ə **about**
ā	ape	ē	me	ō	old	ū	use	ng **song**	taken
ä	far	i	it	ôr	fork	ü	rule	th **thin**	pencil
âr	care	ī	ice	oi	oil	ù	pull	<u>th</u> **this**	lemon
ô	law	îr	pierce	ou	out	ûr	turn	zh **measure**	circus

′ = primary accent; shows which syllable takes the main stress, such as **kil** in **kilogram** (kil′ə gram′).
′ = secondary accent; shows which syllables take lighter stresses, such as **gram** in **kilogram**.

B

bacteria, (bak tîr′ē ə) One-celled living things. (p. B18)

barometer (bə rom′i tər) A device for measuring air pressure. (p. D24)

bird (bûrd) An animal that has a beak, feathers, two wings, and two legs. (p. A73)

bulb (bulb) The underground stem of such plants as onions and irises. (p. A30)

C

camouflage (kam′ə fläzh) An adaptation that allows animals to blend into their surroundings. (p. B52)

carbon dioxide and oxygen cycles (kär′bən dī ok′sīd and ok′sə jən sī′kəlz) The process of passing oxygen and carbon dioxide from one population to another in both water and land habitats. (p. B27)

carnivore (kär′nə vôr′) An animal that eats only other animals. (p. B20)

cast (kast) A fossil formed or shaped inside a mold. (p. C23)

cell (sel) **1.** The basic building block of life. (p. A10) **2.** A source of electricity. (p. F72)

cell membrane (sel mem′brān′) The thin outer covering of a cell. (p. A10)

cell wall (sel wôl) A stiff layer outside the cell membrane of plant cells. (p. A11)

chemical change (kəm′i kəl chānj) A change that forms a different kind of matter. (p. F30)

chloroplast (klôr′ə plast′) One of the small green bodies inside a plant cell that makes foods for the plant. (p. A11)

circuit (sûr′kit) The path electricity flows through. (p. F72)

classify (klas′ə fī) To place materials that share properties together in groups. (pp. S3, A66)

communicate (kə mü′ni kāt′) To share information. (pp. S11, F20)

community (kə mü′ni tē) All the living things in an ecosystem. (p. B6)

competition (kom′pi tish′ən) The struggle among organisms for water, food, or other needs. (p. B42)

compound (kom′pound) Two or more elements put together. (p. F30)

compound machine (kom′pound mə shēn′) Two or more simple machines put together. (p. E57)

condense (kən dens′) *v.* To change from a gas to a liquid. (pp. C31, F17) —**condensation** (kon′den sā′shən) *n.* (p. D17)

conductor (kən duk′tər) A material that heat travels through easily. (p. F46)

conifer (kon′ə fər) A tree that produces seeds inside of cones. (p. A28)

conserve (kən sûrv′) To save, protect, or use something wisely without wasting it. (p. C34)

consumer (kən sü′mər) An organism that eats producers or other consumers. (pp. A40, B17)

crater (krā′tər) A hollow area in the ground. (p. D49)

cutting (kut′ing) A plant part from which a new plant can grow. (p. A30)

cytoplasm (sī′tə pla′zəm) A clear, jellylike material that fills both plant and animal cells. (p. A10)

D

decibel (dB) (des′ə bel′) A unit that measures loudness. (p. F69)

decomposer (dē′kəm pō′zər) An organism that breaks down dead plant and animal material. *Decomposers* recycle chemicals so they can be used again. (p. B18)

define based on observations (di fīn′ bāst ôn ob′zər vā′shənz) To put together a description that relies on examination and experience. (p. S5)

degree (di grē′) The unit of measurement for temperature. (p. F43)

PRONUNCIATION KEY

a at; ā ape; ä far; âr care; ô law; e end; ē me; i it; ī ice; îr pierce; o hot; ō old; ôr fork; oi oil; ou out; u up; ū use; ü rule; u̇ pull; ûr turn; hw white; ng song; th thin; <u>th</u> this; zh measure; ə about, taken, pencil, lemon, circus

desert (dez′ərt) A hot, dry place with very little rain. (p. B55)

development (di vel′əp mənt) The way a living thing changes during its life. (p. A6)

distance (dis′təns) The length between two places. (p. E7)

E

earthquake (ûrth′kwāk) A sudden movement in the rocks that make up Earth's crust. (p. C72)

ecosystem (ek′ō sis′təm) All the living and nonliving things in an environment and all their interactions. (p. B6)

electric current (i lek′trik kûr′ənt) Electricity that flows through a circuit. (p. F72)

element (el′ə mənt) A building block of matter. (p. F28)

embryo (em′brē ō) A young organism that is just beginning to grow. (p. A26)

endangered (en dān′jərd) Close to becoming extinct; having very few of its kind left. (p. B64)

energy (en′ər jē) The ability to do work. (pp. A18, E39)

energy pyramid (en′ər jē pir′ə mid′) A diagram that shows how energy is used in an ecosystem. (p. B22)

environment (en vī′rən mənt) The things that make up an area, such as land, water, and air. (p. A8)

erosion (i rō′zhən) The carrying away of weathered materials. (p. C62)

evaporate (i vap′ə rāt′) v. To change from a liquid to a gas. (pp. C31, F17) —**evaporation** (i vap′ə rā′shən′) n. (p. D17)

experiment (ek sper′ə ment′) To perform a test to support or disprove a hypothesis. (pp. S7, A12)

extinct (ek stingkt) Died out, leaving no more of that type of organism alive. (p. B66)

F

fertilizer (fûr′tə līz) A substance added to the soil that is used to make plants grow. (p. C42)

first quarter (fûrst kwôr′tər) A phase of the Moon in which the right half is visible and growing larger. (p. D47)

fish (fish) An animal that lives its whole life in water. (p. A71)

flood (flud) A great rush of water over usually dry land. (p. C71)

flowering plant (flou'ər ing plant) A plant that produces seeds inside of flowers. (p. A28)

fog (fôg) A cloud that forms near the ground. (p. D14)

food chain (füd chān) A series of organisms that depend on one another for food. (p. B17)

food web (füd web) Several food chains that are connected. (p. B20)

force (fôrs) A push or pull, such as the one that moves a lever. (pp. E14, E44)

form a hypothesis (fôrm ə hī poth'ə sis) To make a statement that can be tested in answer to a question. (pp. S5, C64)

fossil (fos'əl) The imprint or remains of something that lived long ago. (p. C22)

freeze (frēz) To turn from water to ice. (p. F17)

friction (frik'shən) A force that occurs when one object rubs against another. (p. E26)

fuel (fū'əl) A substance burned for its energy. (p. C26)

fulcrum (fùl'krəm) The point where a lever turns or pivots. (p. E44)

full Moon (fùl mün) or **second quarter** (sek'ənd kwôr'tər) The phase of the Moon in which all of its sunlit half is visible from Earth. (p. D47)

fungi, (fun'jī) *pl. n., sing.* **fungus** (fung'gəs) One- or many-celled organisms that absorb food from dead organisms. (p. B18)

G

gas (gas) Matter that has no definite shape or volume. (p. F14)

PRONUNCIATION KEY

a at; ā ape; ä far; âr care; ô law; e end; ē me; i it; ī ice; îr pierce; o hot; ō old; ôr fork; oi oil; ou out; u up; ū use; ü rule; ù pull; ûr turn; hw white; ng song; th thin; <u>th</u> this; zh measure; ə about, taken, pencil, lemon, circus

germinate (jûr′mə nāt) To begin to grow, as when the right conditions allow a seed to develop. (p. A26)

glacier (glā′shər) A large mass of ice in motion. (p. C62)

gram (gram) A metric unit used to measure mass; 1,000 *grams* equals 1 kilogram. (p. F9)

gravity (grav′i tē) A pulling force between two objects, such as Earth and you. (p. E16)

groundwater (ground wô′tər) Water stored in the cracks of underground rocks and soil. (p. C33)

H

habitat (hab′i tat) The home of a living thing. (p. B7)

heat (hēt) A form of energy that makes things warmer. (p. F42)

herbivore (hûr′bə vôr′) An animal that eats only plants. (p. B20)

heredity (hə red′i tē) The passing of traits from parents to offspring. (p. A27)

hibernate (hī′bər nāt′) To rest or sleep through the cold winter. (p. A46)

host (hōst) An organism that a parasite lives with. (p. B31)

humus (hü′məs) Leftover decomposed plant and animal matter. (p. C14)

hurricane (hûr′i kān′) A violent storm with strong winds and heavy rains. (p. C70)

I

igneous rock (ig′nē əs rok) A "fire-made" rock formed from melted rock material. (p. C8)

imprint (im′print′) A shallow mark or print in a rock. (p. C23)

inclined plane (in klīnd′ plān) A flat surface that is raised at one end. (p. E54)

infer (in fûr′) To form an idea from facts or observations. (pp. S5, D20)

inherited trait (in her′i təd trāt) A characteristic that comes from parents. (p. A56)

inner planet (in'ər plan'it) Any of the four planets in the solar system that are closest to the Sun: Mercury, Venus, Earth, and Mars. (p. D56)

insulator (in'sə lā'tər) A material that heat doesn't travel through easily. (p. F46)

interpret data (in tûr'prit dā'tə) To use the information that has been gathered to answer questions or solve a problem. (p. S9)

K

key (kē) A table that shows what different symbols on a map stand for. (p. E10)

kilogram (kil'ə gram') A metric unit used to measure mass; 1 *kilogram* equals 1,000 grams. (p. F9)

L

landform (land'fôrm') A feature on Earth's surface. (p. C54)

last quarter (last kwôr'tər) or **third quarter** (thûrd kwôr'tər) The phase of the waning Moon in which the left half is visible but growing smaller. (p. D47)

leaf (lēf) A plant part that grows from the stem and helps the plant get air and make food. (p. A18)

learned trait (lûrnd trāt) Something that you are taught or learn from experience. (p. A56)

lens (lenz) A curved piece of glass. (p. D58)

lever (lev'ər) A straight bar that moves on a fixed point. (p. E44)

life cycle (līf sī'kəl) All the stages in an organism's life. (p. A26)

liquid (lik'wid) Matter that has a definite volume but not a definite shape. (p. F14)

liter (lē'tər) A metric unit used to measure volume. (p. F9)

load (lōd) The object that a lever lifts or moves. (p. E44)

PRONUNCIATION KEY

a at; ā ape; ä far; âr care; ô law; e end; ē me; i it; ī ice; îr pierce; o hot; ō old; ôr fork; oi oil; ou out; u up; ū use; ü rule; u̇ pull; ûr turn; hw white; ng song; th thin; th this; zh measure; ə about, taken, pencil, lemon, circus

loam (lōm) A kind of soil that contains clay, sand, silt, and humus. Plants grow well in loam. (p. C15)

luster (lus′tər) How an object reflects light. (p. F6)

M

machine (mə shēn′) A tool that makes work easier to do. (p. E44)

magnetism (mag′ni tiz′əm) The property of an object that makes it attract iron. (p. F26)

make a model (māk ə mod′əl) To make something to represent an object or event. (p. S7)

mammal (mam′əl) An animal with fur that feeds its young with milk. (p. A74)

map (map) A flat drawing that shows the positions of things. (p. E10)

mass (mas) The amount of matter in an object. (p. F7)

matter (mat′ər) Anything that takes up space and has mass. (pp. D16, F6)

measure (mezh′ər) To find the size, volume, area, mass, weight, or temperature of an object, or how long an event occurs. (pp. S9, C16)

melt (melt) To change from a solid to a liquid. (p. F17)

metal (met′əl) A shiny material found in the ground. (p. F26)

metamorphic rock (met′ə môr′fik rok) A rock that has changed form through squeezing and heating. (p. C9)

metamorphosis (met′ə môr′fə sis) A change in the body form of an organism. (p. A52)

microscope (mī′krə skōp′) A device that uses glass lenses to allow people to see very small things. (p. A10)

migrate (mī′grāt) To move to another place. (p. A46)

mimicry (mim′i krē) The imitation by one animal of the traits of another. (p. B53)

mineral (min′ə rəl) A naturally occurring substance, neither plant nor animal. (pp. A16, C6)

mixture (miks'chər) Different types of matter mixed together. The properties of each kind of matter in the mixture do not change. (p. F18)

mold (mold) An empty space in a rock that once contained an object such as a dead organism. (p. C23)

motion (mō'shən) A change in position. (p. E8)

mountain (moun'tən) The highest of Earth's landforms. *Mountains* often have steep sides and pointed tops. (p. C55)

N

natural resource (nach'ər əl rē'sôrs') A material on Earth that is necessary or useful to people. (p. C38)

nectar (nek'tər) The sugary liquid in flowers that lures insects that aid in pollination. (p. A28)

new Moon (nü mün) A phase of the Moon in which none of its sunlit half is visible from Earth. (p. D47)

newton (nü'tən) The unit used to measure pushes and pulls. (pp. E17, F10)

niche (nich) The job or role an organism has in an ecosystem. (p. B44)

nonrenewable resource (non'ri nü'ə bəl rē'sôrs') A resource that cannot be reused or replaced easily. (p. C41)

nucleus (nü'klē əs) The control center of a cell. (p. A11)

O

observe (əb sûrv') To use one or more of the senses to identify or learn about an object or event. (pp. S3, B56)

omnivore (om'nə vôr') An animal that eats both plants and animals. (p. B21)

PRONUNCIATION KEY

a at; ā ape; ä far; âr care; ô law; e end; ē me; i it; ī ice; îr pierce; o hot; ō old; ôr fork; oi oil; ou out; u up; ū use; ü rule; ů pull; ûr turn; hw white; ng song; th thin; th this; zh measure; ə about, taken, pencil, lemon, circus

opaque (ō pāk´) A material that doesn't allow light to pass through. (p. F54)

orbit (ôr´bit) The path an object follows as it revolves around another object. (p. D38)

organ (ôr´gən) A group of tissues that work together. (p. A62)

organism (ôr´gə niz´əm) Any living thing. (p. A6)

outer planet (out´ər plan´it) Any of the five planets in the solar system that are farthest from the Sun: Jupiter, Saturn, Uranus, Neptune, and Pluto. (p. D56)

oxygen (ok´sə jən) A gas that is in air and water. (p. A19)

P

parasite (par´ə sīt´) An organism that lives in or on a host. (p. B31)

perish (per´ish) To fail to survive. (p. B63)

phase (fāz) An apparent change in the Moon's shape. (p. D46)

physical change (fiz´i kəl chānj) A change in the way matter looks that leaves the matter itself unchanged. (p. F16)

pitch (pich) How high or low a sound is. (p. F66)

plain (plān) Wide, flat lands. (p. C55)

planet (plan´it) Any of the nine large bodies that orbit the Sun. In order from the Sun outward, they are Mercury, Venus, Earth, Mars, Jupiter, Saturn, Uranus, Neptune, and Pluto. (p. D54)

pollen (pol´ən) A powdery material needed by the eggs of flowers to make seeds. (p. A28)

pollution (pə lü´shən) The adding of harmful substances to the water, air, or land. (p. C42)

population (pop´yə lā´shən) All the members of a single type of organism in an ecosystem. (p. B6)

position (pə zish´ən) The location of an object. (p. E6)

precipitation (pri sip´i tā´shən) Water in the atmosphere that falls to Earth as rain, snow, hail, or sleet. (p. D19)

predator (pred'ə tər) An animal that hunts other animals for food. (p. B28)

predict (pri dikt') To state possible results of an event or experiment. (pp. S7, D50)

prey (prā) The animals that predators eat. (p. B28)

prism (pri'zəm) A thick piece of glass that refracts light. (p. F57)

producer (prə dü'sər) An organism such as a plant that makes its own food. (p. B16)

property (prop'ər tē) Any characteristic of matter that you can observe. (p. F6)

pulley (pül'ē) A simple machine that uses a wheel and a rope. (p. E48)

R

rain gauge (rān gāj) A device that measures how much precipitation has fallen. (p. D24)

ramp (ramp) Another name for an inclined plane. (p. E54)

recycle (rē sī'kəl) To treat something so it can be used again. (p. C44)

reduce (ri düs') To use less of something. (p. C44)

reflect (ri flekt') The bouncing of light off a surface. (p. F55)

refract (ri frakt') The bending of light as it passes through matter. (p. F56)

relocate (rē lō'kāt) To find a new home. (p. B63)

renewable resource (ri nü'ə bəl rē'sôrs') A resource that can be replaced or used over and over again. (p. C40)

reproduction (rē'prə duk'shən) The way organisms make more of their own kind. (p. A7)

reptile (rep'təl') An animal that lives on land and has waterproof skin. (p. A72)

PRONUNCIATION KEY

a at; ā ape; ä far; âr care; ô law; e end; ē me; i it; ī ice; îr pierce; o hot; ō old; ôr fork; oi oil; ou out; u up; ū use; ü rule; ú pull; ûr turn; hw white; ng song; th thin; th this; zh measure; ə about, taken, pencil, lemon, circus

reservoir (rez'ər vwär') A storage area for fresh water supplies. (p. C32)

respond (ri spond') To react to changes in the environment. (p. A8)

reuse (rē ūz') To use something again. (p. C44)

revolve (ri volv') To move around another object. (p. D38)

river (riv'ər) A large stream of water that flows across the land. (p. C55)

root (rüt) A plant part that takes in water and grows under the ground. (p. A17)

rotate (rō'tāt) To turn around. (p. D36)

S

sand dune (sand dün) A mound of windblown sand. (p. C55)

sapling (sap'ling) A very young tree. (p. A6)

satellite (sat'ə līt') Any object that orbits another larger body in space. (p. D46)

scavenger (skav'ən jər) An animal that gets its food by eating dead organisms. (p. B29)

screw (skrü) An inclined plane wrapped into a spiral. (p. E56)

sedimentary rock (sed'ə men'tə rē rok) A kind of rock formed when sand, mud, or pebbles at the bottom of rivers, lakes, and oceans pile up. (p. C8)

seedling (sēd'ling) A young plant. (p. A27)

shelter (shel'tər) A place or object that protects an animal and keeps it safe. (p. A44)

simple machine (sim'pəl mə shēn') A machine with few or no moving parts. (p. E44)

soil (soil) A mixture of tiny rock particles, minerals, and decayed plant and animal materials. (p. C14)

solar system (sō'lər sis'təm) The Sun and all the objects that orbit the Sun. (p. D54)

solid (sol'id) Matter that has a definite shape and volume. (p. F14)

solution (sə lū'shən) A kind of mixture in which one or more types of matter are mixed evenly in another type of matter. (p. F19)

speed (spēd) How fast an object moves over a certain distance. (p. E9)

sphere (sfîr) A body that has the shape of a ball or globe. (p. D36)

spore (spôr) One of the tiny reproductive bodies of ferns and mosses, similar to the seeds of other plants. (p. A30)

star (stär) A huge, hot sphere of gases, like the Sun, that gives off its own light. (p. D55)

stem (stem) A plant part that supports the plant. (p. A17)

switch (swich) A lever that opens or closes an electric circuit. (p. F73)

system (sis'təm) A group of parts that work together. (p. A62)

telescope (tel'ə skōp') A tool that gathers light to make faraway objects appear closer. (p. D58)

temperature (tem'pər ə cher) How hot or cold something is. (pp. D8, F43)

texture (teks'chər) How the surface of an object feels to the touch. (p. F6)

thermometer (thər mom'ə tər) An instrument used to measure temperature. (pp. D8, D24)

tissue (tish'ü) A group of cells that are alike. (p. A62)

tornado (tôr nā'dō) A violent, whirling wind that moves across the ground in a narrow path. (p. C70)

tuber (tü'bər) The underground stem of a plant such as the potato. (p. A30)

tundra (tun'drə) A cold, dry place. (p. B55)

PRONUNCIATION KEY

a at; ā ape; ä far; âr care; ô law; e end; ē me; i it; ī ice; îr pierce; o hot; ō old; ôr fork; oi oil; ou out; u up; ū use; ü rule; u̇ pull; ûr turn; hw white; ng song; th thin; <u>th</u> this; zh measure; ə about, taken, pencil, lemon, circus

use numbers (ūz num′bərz) To order, count, add, subtract, multiply, or divide to explain data. (p. S9)

use variables (ūz vâr′ē ə bəlz) To identify and separate things in an experiment that can be changed or controlled. (pp. S7, F58)

valley (val′ē) An area of low land lying between hills or mountains. (p. C55)

vibrate (vī′brāt) To move back and forth quickly. (p. F64)

volcano (vol kā′nō) An opening in the surface of Earth. (p. C73)

volume (vol′ūm) **1.** A measure of how much space matter takes up. (p. F7) **2.** How loud or soft a sound is. (p. F67)

W

water cycle (wô′tər sī′kəl) The movement of Earth's water over and over from a liquid to a gas and from a gas to a liquid. (pp. C31, D19)

water vapor (wô′tər vā′pər) Water in the form of a gas in Earth's atmosphere. (p. D17)

weather (weth′ər) The condition of the atmosphere at a given time and place. (p. D6)

weather vane (weth′ər vān) A device that indicates the direction of the wind. (p. D25)

weathering (weth′ər ing) The process that causes rocks to crumble, crack, and break. (p. C60)

wedge (wej) Two inclined planes placed back-to-back. (p. E55)

weight (wāt) The measure of the pull of gravity between an object and Earth. (p. E17)

wheel and axle (hwēl and ak′səl) A wheel that turns on a post. (p. E47)

wind (wind) Moving air. (p. D10)

windlass (wind′ləs) A wheel and axle machine that is turned by a hand crank to lift a bucket in a well. (p. E47)

work (wûrk) The force that changes the motion of an object. (p. E38)

Index

* Indicates an activity related to this topic.

* Indicates an activity related to this topic.

* Indicates an activity related to this topic.

* Indicates an activity related to this topic.

* Indicates an activity related to this topic.

Credits

Cover Photos: c. Leeson Photography; bkgd. Roderick Chen/Superstock; spine Leeson Photography. Back Cover: bkgd. Roderick Chen/Superstock; t.l. Clive Druett/Papilio/CORBIS; t.r. Tim Flach/Stone/Getty Images; c.l. Donovan Reese/Stone/Getty Images; c.r. Earth Satellite Corporation/Science Photo Library/Photo Researchers, Inc.; b.l. James Marshall/The Stock Market/CORBIS; b.r. SuperStock. Endpaper: Roderick Chen/Superstock.

Photography Credits: All photos are by Macmillan/McGraw-Hill (MMH) and Ken Karp for MMH, Ray Boudreau for MMH, Dan Howell for MMH, David Waitz for MMH, Ron Tanaka for MMH, Dave Mager for MMH, Richard Hutchings for MMH and John Serafin for MMH except as noted below:

i: bkgd. Roderick Chen/Superstock; t.l, b.l. Leeson Photography. iii: Leeson Photography. iv: t. NASA/CORBIS; c., b. Courtesy Sally Ride; bkgd. Taxi/Getty Images. v: l. Mervyn Rees/Alamy; r. James L. Amos/CORBIS. vi: l. Victoria McCormick/Animals Animals; b. PhotoDisc/Getty Images. vii: l. inset Tim Davis/Stone/Getty Images; l. bkgd. Christer Fredriksson/Natural Selection Stock Photography, Inc.; b. Runk/Schoenberger/Grant Heilman Photography, Inc.; ants PhotoDisc/Getty Images. viii: l. Donovan Reese/Stone/Getty Images; b.c. Francois Gohier/Photo Researchers, Inc.; b.r. American Museum of Natural History. ix: l. Earth Satellite Corporation/Science Photo Library/Photo Researchers, Inc.; c. NASA/Photo Researchers, Inc.; r. John Sanford/Photo Researchers, Inc. x: l. Ron Stroud/Masterfile; b. Peter Weimann/Animals Animals/Earth Scenes. xi: l. Superstock; r. D. Boone/CORBIS. xiv: l. Roderick Chen/Superstock. xvi: b.r.: PhotoDisc/Getty Images. SO: Danny Lehman/CORBIS. S0-S1: James L. Amos/CORBIS. S2-S3: Tom Bean/CORBIS. S4: Mervyn Rees/Alamy. S5: DK Images. S6-S7: Ira Block/National Geographic. S8-S9: Robert Campbell/CORBIS. S10-S11: Richard Cummins/CORBIS. AO: Clive Druett/Papilio/CORBIS. A2: Victoria McCormick/Animals Animals. A2-A3: Alan Oddie/PhotoEdit. A4-A5: Douglas Peebles/CORBIS. A6: l. Tony Wharton/The Stock Market/CORBIS; t., b. Terry Eggers/The Stock Market/CORBIS; r. The Stock Market/CORBIS. A6-A7: Frank Siteman/Stock Boston. A7: PhotoDisc/Getty Images. A8: t. Gerard Fuehrer/DRK Photo; b. SuperStock. A9: t. Norbert Wu/Peter Arnold, Inc.; c. Secret Sea Visions/Peter Arnold, Inc.; b. Joe McDonald/Visuals Unlimited, Inc. A10: t. Kent Wood/Photo Researchers, Inc.; b. Dwight R. Kuhn. A11: Moredun Animal Health LTD/Science Photo Library/Photo Researchers, Inc. A13: Carl Roessler/Animals Animals/Earth Scenes. A14: t.l. Doug Peebles/Panoramic Images; r. Mark Segal/Panoramic Images. A14-A15: bkgd. Ryan McVay/PhotoDisc/Getty Images; c. Allen Prier/Panoramic Images. A16: bkgd. Runk/Schoenberger/Grant Heilman Photography; inset E. Webber/Visuals Unlimited. A17: b. Jim Zipp/Photo Researchers, Inc.; r. Jenny Hager/The Image Works. A18: l. Runk/Schoenberger/Grant Heilman Photography; r. C.G. Van Dyke/Visuals Unlimited. A19: t. Dave M. Phillips/Visuals Unlimited. A20: l. Bill Beatty/Visuals Unlimited; b. Pat O'Hara/DRK Photo. A22: l. Stan Osolinski/Dembinsky Photo Associates; r. Larry West/Taxi/Getty Images. A22-A23: Randy Green/Taxi/Getty Images. A23: t. John M. Roberts/The Stock Market/CORBIS; b. J. H. Robinson/Photo Researchers, Inc. A24-A25: Neil Gilchrist/Panoramic Images. A26: t. D. Gavagnaro/Visuals Unlimited; t.c.r. Kevin Collins/Visuals Unlimited; c.r. Tony Freeman/PhotoEdit; b. Inga Spence/Tom Stack & Associates. A26-A27: Inga Spence/Visuals Unlimited. A27: D. Gavagnaro/Visuals Unlimited. A29: Gerald and Buff Corsi/Visuals Unlimited. A30: t., c. David Young-Wolff/PhotoEdit; b.l. Ed Reschke/Peter Arnold, Inc.; b.r. Jeff J. Daly/Visuals Unlimited. A32: Ed Galindo. A32-A33: l., c., t. Ed Galindo; b.r. C Squared Studios/PhotoDisc/Getty Images. A36-A37: Stephen J. Krasemann/Photo Researchers, Inc. A38-A39: Jade Albert/FPG International/Getty Images. A40: t. Fritz Polikng/Bruce Coleman, Inc.; b.l. Joe McDonald/DRK Photo; b.r. Dale E. Boyer/Photo Researchers, Inc. A41: Kevin Schafer/Peter Arnold, Inc. A42: inset W. Gregory Brown/Animals Animals. A42-A43: Michael S. Nolan/Tom Stack & Associates. A44: t. Eric & David Hosking/CORBIS; c. John Cancalosi/DRK Photo; b. Ted Levine/Animals Animals. A45: t. Zoran Milich/Allsport USA/Getty Images; b. Mark Newman/Bruce Coleman, Inc. A 46: t. David Madison/Bruce Coleman, Inc.; c. Runk/Schoenberger/Grant Heilman Photography; b. John Cancalosi/DRK Photo. A48: t. Robert P. Carr/Bruce Coleman, Inc.; b. Skip Moody/Dembinsky Photo Associates. A48-A49: Ken Lucas/Visuals Unlimited. A49: t.l., t.r., b. Robert P. Carr/Bruce Coleman, Inc.; c. Jon Dicus. A50-A51: Tim Davis/Photo Researchers, Inc. A52: t. Dwight R. Kuhn; b. Arthur Morris/Visuals Unlimited. A53: t.l. Gelnn M. Oliver/Visuals Unlimited; t.c. Pat Lynch/Zipp/Photo Researchers, Inc.; t.r. Robert P. Carr/Bruce Coleman, Inc.; c.l. Nuridsany et Perennou/Zipp/Photo Researchers, Inc.; c.r. Robert L. Dunne/Bruce Coleman, Inc.; b.l. Sharon Cummings/Dembinsky Photo Associates; b.r. John Mielcarek/Dembinsky Photo Associates. A54: t. SuperStock; c. Lynn Rogers/Peter Arnold, Inc.; b .l. Erwin and Peggy Bauer/Bruce Coleman, Inc.; b.r. Pat

and Tom Leeson/Photo Researchers, Inc. A55: t.l. Cabisco/Visuals Unlimited; t.c.l. E.A. Janes/Bruce Coleman, Inc.; t.r. Lindholm/Visuals Unlimited; b.c.l. Fred Breummer/DRK Photo; b.r. Dave B. Fleetham/Visuals Unlimited; b.l. M H Sharp/Photo Researchers, Inc. A56: l. George Shelley/The Stock Market/CORBIS; r. Richard Hutchings/PhotoEdit. A58: Bill Banaszewski/Visuals Unlimited. A58-A59: J.C. Carton/Bruce Coleman, Inc. A60-A61: Robert Maier/Animals Animals. A62: l. M.I. Walker/Science Source/Photo Researchers, Inc. A63: t. R. Dowling/Animals Animals/Earth Scenes; b. Joe McDonald/Animals Animals/Earth Scenes. A64: Robert Winslow. A64-A65: Tom Brakefield/CORBIS. A65: t. James Watt/Animals Animals/Earth Scenes; b. Jeff Rotman/Jeff Rotman Photography. A66: PhotoDisc/Getty Images. A68-A69: VCG/FPG International/Getty Images. A69: t.r. Stephen Dalton/Animals Animals/Earth Scenes; t.c.r. Tony Wharton/CORBIS; b.c.r. Brian Parker/Tom Stack & Associates; b.r. Lisa and Mike Husar/DRK Photo; c.l. EyeWire; b.l. Kichen and Hurst/Tom Stack & Associates; c. G.W.Willis/Animals Animals/Earth Scenes. A70: l. Darryl Torckler/Stone/Getty Images; r. Rob Simpson/Visuals Unlimited. A71: t. Breck P. Kent/Animals Animals/Earth Scenes; inset George Bernard/Animals Animals/Earth Scenes. A72: t. Jane Burton/Bruce Coleman, Inc.; b. E.R. Degginger/Animals Animals/Earth Scenes. A73: l. S. Nielson/DRK Photo; r. Robert Winslow. A74: Jeff Rotman/Jeff Rotman Photography. A74-A75: Dave Watts/Tom Stack & Associates. A75: t. Erwin & Peggy Bauer/Bruce Coleman, Inc.; b. Lynn M. Stone/Bruce Coleman Inc. A77: SuperStock. A78: Photo courtesy of Dan Lausser/University of Wisconsin-Madison. A78-A79: c. Photo courtesy Jeff Miller/University of Wisconsin-Madison; bkgd. StockTrek/Photodisc Green/Getty Images. A80: l. Jeff J. Daly/Visuals Unlimited; r. David Young-Wolff/PhotoEdit. BO: Tim Flach/Stone/Getty Images. B0-B1: Christer Fredriksson/Natural Selection Stock Photography. B1: Tim Davis/Stone/Getty Images. B2-B3: Raymond Gehman/CORBIS. B4-B5: Johnny Johnson/Animals Animals/Earth Scenes. B5: PhotoDisc/Getty Images. B6: Nicholas DeVore/Stone/Getty Images. B6-B7: Joseph Van Os/The Image Bank/Getty Images. B12: inset Lance Nelson/The Stock Market/CORBIS; c. Jeff Greenberg/Visuals Unlimited; b. Jeff Greenberg/PhotoEdit. B13: t. Gerard Lacz/Peter Arnold, Inc.; b. PhotoDisc/Getty Images. B14-B15: L. Lenz/Natural Selection. B16: t. Kim Taylor/Dorling Kindersley Ltd. B18: t. SuperStock; b.l. Michael P. Gadomski/Photo Researchers, Inc. B18-B19: Dwight Kuhn Photography. B22: t. John Warden/Stone/Getty Images; t.c. Tom J. Ulrich/Visuals Unlimited; b.c. John Shaw/Bruce Coleman, Inc.; b. Runk/Schoenberger/Grant Heilman Photography, Inc. B24-B25: Michael Simpson/FPG International/Getty Images. B26: William H. Mullins/Photo Researchers, Inc. B26-B27: bkgd. Kent Foster/Photo Researchers, Inc. B28: t. Kim Taylor/Dorling Kindersley Ltd.; c. John Shaw/Bruce Coleman, Inc.; branch Kim Taylor/Dorling Kindersley Ltd.; b. Arthur Morris/The Stock Market/CORBIS. B28-B29: inset Kim Taylor/Dorling Kindersley Ltd.; bkgd. M. C. Chamberlain/DRK Photo. B29: t. Jeremy Woodhouse/PhotoDisc/Getty Images; b. Jerry Young/Dorling Kindersley Ltd. B30: t. Nawrocki Stock Photo; b. Carl Roessler/Bruce Coleman, Inc. B30-B31: S. Dimmitt/Photo Researchers, Inc. B31: t. James H. Robinson/Photo Researchers, Inc.; b.l. Patricia Doyle/Stone/Getty Images; b.r. Runk/Schoenberger/Grant Heilman Photography, Inc. B32-B33: Kim Taylor/Dorling Kindersley Ltd. B34: l. Trevor Barrett/Animals Animals/Earth Scenes; b. George D. Lepp/Photo Researchers, Inc. B34-B35: John Elk III. B35: Kjell B. Sandved/Visuals Unlimited. B37: l., c. Runk/Schoenberger/Grant Heilman Photography, Inc.; r. Arthur Morris/Visuals Unlimited. B38-B39: Robert Winslow. B40-B41: The Stock Market/CORBIS. B42: t. Stephen Dalton/Animals Animals/Earth Scenes; b. Richard Day/Panoramic Images. B43: t.l. Steve Maslowski/Visuals Unlimited; t.r. James P. Rowan/DRK Photo; b.l. George D. Dodge/Bruce Coleman, Inc.; b.r. Michael Dwyer/Stock Boston. B44: t. Gail Shumway/FPG International/Getty Images. B46: Paul McCormick/Getty Images. B47: Gil T Friedman. B48: Richard & Susan Day/Animals Animals/Earth Scenes. B48-B49: bkgd. Johnny Johnson/Animals Animals/Earth Scenes; c. Tom and Pat Leeson/DRK Photo. B50: t. Gail Shumway/FPG International/Getty Images; c. Jack Jeffrey/Photo Resource Hawaii; b. John Cancalosi/DRK Photo. B50-B51: t. Francis/Donna Caldwell/Visuals Unlimited; b. Kim Taylor/Bruce Coleman, Inc. B51: Heather Angel/Natural Visions. B52: t. Gregory Ochoki/Photo Researchers, Inc.; b. Breck P. Kent/Animals Animals/Earth Scenes. B53: t. Stephen J. Krasemann/DRK Photo; b.l. John Eastcott/Yva Momatiuk/DRK Photo; b.r. A. Cosmos Blank/Photo Researchers, Inc. B54: t. Zig Leszczynski/Animals Animals/Earth Scenes; b. Michael Fogden/DRK Photo. B54-B55: Michael Fogden/DRK Photo. B55: t.l. Pat O'Hara/DRK Photo; t.c. Don Enger/Animals Animals/Earth Scenes; t.r. Richard Kolar/Animals Animals/Earth Scenes; b.l. Jim Steinberg/Photo Researchers, Inc.; b.r. Stephen J. Krasemann/Photo Researchers, Inc. B57: Chris Johns/National Geographic . B58-B59: Gary Braasch/CORBIS. B60: t. Charles Palek/Earth Scenes; b. Pat and Tom Leeson/Photo Researchers, Inc. B60-B61: Brett Baunton. B61: Wayne

Hacker/Alamy. B62: l. Kent and Donna Dannen/Photo Researchers, Inc.; t.r. Diana L. Stratton/Tom Stack & Associates; t.c.r. Doug Sokell/Visuals Unlimited; b.c.r. Sharon Gerig/Tom Stack & Associates; b.r. Pat and Tom Leeson/DRK Photo. B63: t. Joe & Carol McDonald/Visuals Unlimited; b. Stephen J. Krasemann/DRK Photo. B64: t. M.C. Chamberlain/DRK Photo; b.l. Erwin and Peggy Bauer/Bruce Coleman Inc.; b.r. G. Prance/Visuals Unlimited. B65: M.C. Chamberlain/DRK Photo. B66: t. Stephen J. Krasemann/DRK Photo; b. Science VU/Visuals Unlimited. B69: l. Pat and Tom Leeson/Photo Researchers, Inc.; r. Robert Madden/National Geographic . B70: Smithsonian. B70-B71: b. PhotoDisc/Getty Images; bkgd. Cartesia/PhotoDisc. B71: t. Martin Harvey/CORBIS; b. Royalty-Free/CORBIS. CO: Donovan Reese/Stone/ Getty Images. C0-C1: David Muench/Stone/Getty Images. C2-C3: David Muench/CORBIS. C4-C5: Chip Porter/Stone/Getty Images. C6: t. Joyce Photographics/Photo Researchers, Inc.; b.l. Bill Bachmann/Index Stock Imagery; b.r. Runk/Schoenberger/Grant Heilman Photography. C7: t., c. Tom Pantages. C8: Adam G. Sylvester/Photo Researchers, Inc. C9: t.l. Joyce Photographics/Photo Researchers, Inc.; t.r. Runk/Schoenberger/ Grant Heilman Photography; b. Charles R. Belinky/Photo Researchers, Inc. C10: t. Frederik D. Bodin/Stock Boston; c. Erich Lessing/Art Resource; b. Boleslaw Edelhajt/Gamma-Liaison/Getty Images. C12-C13: Bo Brannhage/Panoramic Images. C14-C15: Jeff Lepore/Panoramic Images. C15: l. Stephen Ogilvy for MMH. C17: Runk/Schoenberger/ Grant Heilman Photography. C18: t. The National Archives/CORBIS; b. G. Buttner/Okapia/Photo Researchers, Inc.; inset, c.r. Roy Morsch/The Stock Market/CORBIS. C19: bkgd. Arthur C. Smith/Grant Heilman Photography; t. Roy Morsch/The Stock Market/CORBIS. C20-C21: bkgd. Jeff J. Daly/Visuals Unlimited. C22: Tom Bean/DRK Photo. C23: t. Runk/ Schoenberger/Grant Heilman Photography. C24: t. Louis Psihoyos/ MATRIX; inset Mehau Kulyk/Photo Researchers, Inc.; b. Francois Gohier/Photo Researchers, Inc. C24-C25: Biophoto Associates/Photo Researchers, Inc. C25: Stephen J. Krasemann/DRK Photo. C26: Ray Ellis/Photo Researchers, Inc. C28-C29: F. Stuart Westmorland/Photo Researchers, Inc. C30-C31: Tom Van Sant/Photo Researchers, Inc. C32: t. Davis Barber/PhotoEdit; b. C.C. Lockwood/DRK Photo. C36-C37: Grant Heilman/Grant Heilman Photography. C38: Emma Lee/Life File/PhotoDisc/Getty Images. C38-C39: t. David R. Frazier/Photo Researchers, Inc.; b. Charles Mauzy/Natural Selection. C39: John Elk III. C40: t. Don and Pat Valenti/DRK Photo; b. Gary Gray/DRK Photo. C41: t. American Museum of Natural History; inset Will and Deni McIntyre/ Photo Researchers, Inc.; b. George Gerster/Photo Researchers, Inc. C42: t. Ruth Dixon/Stock Boston; b. David Ulmer/Stock Boston. C42-C43: Simon Fraser/Science Photo Library/Photo Researchers, Inc. C44: t.l. Larry Lefever/Grant Heilman Photography; t.c.l. EyeWire; b.c.l. RJ Erwin/DRK Photo; b.l., b.r. Tony Freeman/PhotoEdit. C46: t. David Young-Wolff/PhotoEdit; b. Chromosohm/Sohm/Stock Boston. C47: t. Spencer Grant/PhotoEdit; b. Bonnie Kaman/PhotoEdit. C50-C51: Addison Geary/Stock Boston. C52-C53: Allen Prier/Panoramic Images. C53: t. Peter Miller/Panoramic Images; t.c. Richard Sisk/Panoramic Images; c. Mark Heifner/Panoramic Images; b.c. Kim Heacox/Stone/ Getty Images; b.r. Don Pitcher/Stock Boston; b.l. Jack Krawczyk/ Panoramic Images. C56: t.l. Jim Wiebe/Panoramic Images; t.r. Peter Pearson/Stone/Getty Images; b.l. Richard Sisk/Panoramic Images; b.c. Mark Heifner/Panoramic Images; b.r. Tom Bean/Stone/Getty Images. C57: t. Jack Krawczyk/Panoramic Images. C58-C59: David L. Brown/ Panoramic Images. C60: t. Michael P. Gadomski/Photo Researchers, Inc.; b. John Anderson/Animals Animals/Earth Scenes. C62: t. Thomas Fletcher/Stock Boston; inset PhotoDisc/Getty Images; b. Jeff Greenberg/PhotoEdit. C63: t. Kathy Ferguson/PhotoEdit; b. Runk/ Schoenberger/Grant Heilman Photography. C65: PhotoEdit. C66: Adam Jones/Photo Researchers, Inc. C66-C67: The National Archives/CORBIS. C67: t. W. E. Ruth/Bruce Coleman, Inc.; inset Pat Armstrong/Visuals Unlimited; c. Sylvan H. Wittaver/Visuals Unlimited; b. John Sohlden/ Visuals Unlimited. C68-C69: David Young-Wolff/PhotoEdit. C70-C71: t. Ana Laura Gonzalez/Animals Animals/Earth Scenes; b. Mark Montes De Oca/FPG International/Getty Images. C72: t. David Bartruff/FPG International/Getty Images; b. Will & Deni McIntyre/Photo Researchers, Inc. C73: G. Brad Lewis/Stone/Getty Images. C74: t. David Weintraub/Stock Boston; b. Arthur Rothstein/Library of Congress/ Archive Photos/Getty Images. C78: M. Olsen/College of William and Mary. C78-C79: inset Woods Hole Oceanographic Institute; bkgd. Ralph White/CORBIS. DO: bkgd. Earth Satellite Corporation/Science Photo Library/Photo Researchers, Inc. D0: t. John Sanford/Science Photo Library/Photo Researchers, Inc. D0-D1: bkgd. Science Photo Library/Photo Researchers, Inc; inset Photo Library International/Photo Researchers, Inc. D2-D3: Jack Krawczyk/Panoramic Images. D4-D5: Ariel Skelley/The Stock Market/CORBIS. D8-D9: Didier Givois/Photo Researchers, Inc. D10: David Young-Wolff/PhotoEdit. D11: l. Barbara Stotzen/PhotoEdit; r. D. Boone/Corbis. D12: Jim Reed/CORBIS. D13: t. Jim Reed/Photo Researchers, Inc.; b. StockTrek/Photodisc Green/ Getty Images. D14-D15: Clifford Paine/CORBIS. D16: t. Myrleen Ferguson/PhotoEdit; c. Paul Silverman; b. Michael Newman/PhotoEdit. D17: t. Diane Hirsch/Fundamental Photographs; b. Jeff Greenberg/

Peter Arnold, Inc. D21: P. Quittemelle/Stock Boston. D22-D23: Bob Krist/CORBIS. D24: t., b.l. Tom Pantages; b.r. Jeff J. Daly/Stock Boston. D25: t. Charles D. Winters/Photo Researchers, Inc.; b. Tony Freeman/ PhotoEdit. D27: b. NOAA/Science Photo Library/Photo Researchers, Inc. D28: Michael P. Gadomski/Photo Researchers, Inc. D28-D29: F. Stuart Westmorland/Photo Researchers, Inc. D32-D33: Michael Hovell/Index Stock Imagery. D34-D35: Robert Mathena/Fundamental Photographs. D37: t. Ken Lucas/Visuals Unlimited; b. Thomas Barbudo/Panoramic Images. D41: Bob Daemmrich/Stock Boston. D42: Roger Ressmeyer/ CORBIS. D42-D43: Roger Ressmeyer/CORBIS. D43: John Sanford/Photo Network/Alamy. D44-D45: Peter Menzel/Stock Boston. D46: Frank Cara/Bruce Coleman, Inc. D47: John Sanford/Photo Researchers, Inc. D48: NASA/Science Source/Photo Researchers, Inc. D49: l. Mark E. Gibson/Visuals Unlimited; r. NASA/Science Photo Library/Photo Researchers, Inc. D52-D53: Frank Zullo/Photo Researchers, Inc. D56: t. U.S .Geological Survey/Photo Researchers, Inc.; c. NASA/Mark Marten/Photo Researchers, Inc.; b.l. Stock Boston; b.r. NASA/Tom Pantages. D56-D57: Ross Ressmeyer/NASA/CORBIS. D57: t.r. NASA/ Photo Researchers, Inc.; c.l. Space Telescope Space Institute/Photo Researchers, Inc.; c.r. NASA/Tom Pantages; b. Space Telescope Space Institute/Photo Researchers, Inc. D58: t. Tony Freeman/PhotoEdit. D62: t. National Weather Service; c., b. NOAA/AFP/Getty Images. D62-D63: bkgd. Don Farrall/PhotoDisc/Getty Images. D64: b. bkgd. Bruce Heinemann/PhotoDisc/Getty Images. EO: James Marshall/The Stock Market/CORBIS. E0-E1: Ron Stroud/Masterfile. E2-E3: Bernard Asset/Photo Researchers, Inc. E4-E5: S. Dalton/Photo Researchers, Inc. E5: t. Will Hart/PhotoEdit. E6: leaves Foodpix; snails Gregory K. Scott/Photo Researchers, Inc.; b.l., b.r. Zoran Milich/Allsport USA/Getty Images. E8: t. Robert Winslow; b. Fritz Polking/Peter Arnold, Inc. E8-E9: bkgd. The Stock Market/CORBIS. E9: t. Joseph Van Os/The Image Bank/Getty Images; b. Peter Weimann/Animals Animals/Earth Scenes. E12-E13: Craig J. Brown/Flashfocus. E16: l. NASA. E17: NASA/Earth Scenes. E18: PhotoDisc/Getty Images. E19: t. Art Resource. E26: t. Tony Freeman/PhotoEdit; b. John Coletti/Stock Boston. E27: c. Michael Groen for MMH. E30-E31: Dale Sanders/Masterfile. E31: B&C Gill Gillingham/Index Stock Imagery. E34-E35: Addison Geary/Stock Boston. E36-E37: Tom Salyer/Silver Image for MMH. E38: t.l. David Young-Wolff/PhotoEdit; b.r. John Eastcott/Yva Momatiuk/ DRK Photo. E39: David Matherly/Visuals Unlimited. E40: Dan Howell for MMH. E42-E43: Bob Daemmrich/Stock Boston. E46: t. r. Michael Newman/PhotoEdit; c.r. Tony Freeman/PhotoEdit; b.r. Siede Preis/ PhotoDisc/Getty Images. E46-E47: b. Eric Roth/Flashfocus. E47: t. Roger Wilmshurst/Frank Lane Picture Agency/CORBIS; c. CORBIS; b. Eric Roth/Flashfocus . E51: Washington Metropolitan Area Transit Authority. E52-E53: McCutchean/Visuals Unlimited. E54: Richard Hutchings/Photo Researchers, Inc. E55: Donald Specker/Animals Animals/Earth Scenes. E56: Mark Burnett/Stock Boston. E57: t., c. PhotoDisc/Getty Images; b. David Young-Wolff/PhotoEdit. E59: Jodi Jacobson. E62-E63: NASA. E64: b. John Neubauer/PhotoEdit. FO: SuperStock. F0-F1: Kunio Owaki/The Stock Market/CORBIS. F2-F3: Myrleen Ferguson/PhotoEdit. F6: c. C Squared Studios/PhotoDisc/Getty Images; b. PhotoDisc/Getty Images. F6-F7: RDF/Visuals Unlimited. F7: t.l. Spencer Grant/PhotoEdit; t.c. PhotoDisc/Getty Images; t.r. Diane Padys/FPG International/Getty Images; b. Wallace Garrison/Index Stock Imagery. F8: l. Spencer Grant/PhotoEdit; r. Diane Padys/FPG International/Getty Images; r. Stock Boston. F12-F13: Alan Kearney/FPG International/ Getty Images. F14: PhotoDisc/Getty Images. F15: c., r. PhotoDisc/Getty Images. F16: b. David Young-Wolff/PhotoEdit; r., inset Lawrence Migdale . F17: t.l., b.r. SuperStock; t.r. Hutchings Photography; b.l. Amanda Merullo/Stock Boston. F18: t. Dennis Gray/Cole Group/ PhotoDisc/Getty Images. F20: Peter Scoones/TCL/Masterfile. F21: l. Tony Freeman/PhotoEdit. F22: t.c.l. Steve Kline/Bruce Coleman, Inc.; dice Norman Owen Tomalin/Bruce Coleman, Inc. F22-F23: Bruce Byers/ FPG International/Getty Images. F23: t. Norman Owen Tomalin/Bruce Coleman, Inc. F24-F25: Spencer Grant/PhotoEdit. F26-F27: t. Bo Brannhage/Panoramic Images; b. PhotoDisc/Getty Images. F27: t. Burke/Triolo Productions/Foodpix; b. Spike Mafford/PhotoDisc/Getty Images. F28: t. D. Boone/CORBIS. F29: The Stock Market/CORBIS. F30: l. C Squared Studios/PhotoDisc/Getty Images; c. EyeWire; r. Siede Preis/PhotoDisc/Getty Images. F31: c.l. C Squared Studios/PhotoDisc/ Getty Images. F32: t. Ernie Friedlander/Flashfocus/Index Stock Imagery; c.l. Gabriel Covian/The Image Bank/Getty Images; c. Fred J. Maroon/ Photo Researchers, Inc.; c.r. David Sieren/Visuals Unlimited; b.l. Stephen Shepherd/Alamy Images . F34-F35: t. Joel Sartore/Grant Heilman Photography; c. Leonard Lessin/Peter Arnold, Inc.; b. James L. Amos/Peter Arnold, Inc. F35: Gabe Palmer/The Stock Market/CORBIS. F37: l. Tom Pantages; r. Richard Megna/Fundamental Photographs. F38-F39: Glenn Vanstrum/Animals Animals/Earth Scenes. F40: Kim Fennema/Visuals Unlimited. F40-F41: Tom Bean/DRK Photo. F43: b. Bill Bachmann/PhotoEdit. F44-F45: b. Jack Hollingsworth/PhotoDisc/Getty Images. F46: t. Jerry Driendl/FPG International/Getty Images; c. SuperStock; b. Terje Rakke/The Image Bank/Getty Images. F47: